A K-12 educator, principal, and superintendent, perhaps Beth Godett's favorite role has been that of public school teacher. Always a student herself, Dr. Godett earned a law degree after 35 years in the public schools of Pennsylvania, Massachusetts, and New Jersey. She is now an adjunct professor of education law and policy. Dr. Godett has contributed in many ways as an innovative educator. She has been honored as one of the "Women of Inspiration" in Education by the National Association of Women Business Owners; is the recipient of grants through the Carnegie Corporation and the American Society for Quality; and is the force behind business-education partnerships and transformative school initiatives. This is her first book with others now in development.

To teachers—a consequential part of everyone's story making a significant
positive difference in life.

May my book bring affirmation and inspiration.

May you become a major resource and support for colleagues.

Beth Godett

TOWARD THE BIGGER HALF

Equity in Public Education

AUSTIN MACAULEY PUBLISHERS™

LONDON * CAMBRIDGE * NEW YORK * SHARJAH

Ordering Information
Quantity sales: Special discounts are available on quantity purchases by corporations, associations, and others. For details, contact the publisher at the address below.

Publisher's Cataloging-in-Publication data
Godett, Beth
Toward the Bigger Half

ISBN 9798889105039 (Paperback)
ISBN 9798889105046 (ePub e-book)

Library of Congress Control Number: 2023921391

www.austinmacauley.com/us

First Published 2024
Austin Macauley Publishers LLC
40 Wall Street, 33rd Floor, Suite 3302
New York, NY 10005
USA

mail-usa@austinmacauley.com
+1 (646) 5125767

To my husband, Fred—You have always given me the space and encouragement to grow and to be myself without questioning what may sometimes appear to be madness!

To Art Shostak—In the 1980s, you first encouraged me to apply for a Carnegie Grant for High School Improvement to bring a Futures Fair to my district and motivated me to think about the future of public education leading me to my doctoral dissertation. Almost 40 years later, you continue to inspire my work! Your belief in my potential as a writer and your unrelenting support have been foundational in bringing this book to life. Everyone needs a push now and then. Thank you for doing that for me.

To Mike Davis—You have been and continue to be my sounding board and someone on whom I can rely to always ask the hard questions. That we can also speak openly about the delicate issues of race and discrimination has made me a better person and my work more valuable to others (especially my students).

To Keith Plessy and Phoebe Ferguson—Never could I have imagined that a trip to the Final Four in New Orleans would so change my world! You are my connection to history and my catapult into a mission for the future.

To my son, Mike—I can always count on you to indulge my requests for feedback on my writing from the perspective of a respected fellow educator. I hope you know how much your support means to me.

To my son, Joel—You are more of a teacher than you will ever know and have been my cheerleader and my critic in the best of all possible ways. I look forward to your guidance as I take my work to others.

To Tom Welch—my fellow COVID-19 years collaborator. You help me focus on what can be.

To Jana Lee—Your feedback on my drafts has enabled me to see more clearly through your teacher's eyes. I'm glad you're having fun!

To the many who disseminated and completed my survey, listened to my ideas, and provided me with ideas of their own—enormous thanks.

And, to my parents, always part of my work in spirit and by example.

Table of Contents

Abstract

Toward the Bigger Half: Equity in Public Education

An Introduction

This work explores the much-discussed topic of equity in public education. Equity can be elusive, and yet its influence is ever present. It is the bigger half in education—in contrast to equality, which is more of an even split with both sides receiving the same.

It is an enormous challenge to explain an idea that is apt to be seen through many different lenses. Such is the case with equity. Individual perspectives make it hard to define and almost harder to achieve! However, examining equity as a "culture of justice" can provide a more tangible process for articulating what it means and finding ways to bring it to the classroom.

Where and why equity is needed and for whom drive its definition and interpretation. The shift from in-person to virtual learning during the first two years of the COVID-19 pandemic dramatically illustrated how life affords each student unique resources and support systems—some more, some less, but all very dependent upon variables such as wealth, location, and family demographics. It also made clear that every public school and teacher, though facing similar challenges in providing a schooling experience, can encounter vastly different conditions under which to best connect with students and to prepare for doing so.

History and a reckoning of ongoing court cases and legislation show where equity and equality have been attained and where efforts to do so have failed. To think about the relationship between the two, I like to consider the words of a dear colleague who once said that something's being equitable is a concession to its not being equal. True equality may, in fact, be an illusion, something courts have had the power to achieve but, perhaps, neither the conviction nor the perceived independence to do so.

To those intimately involved in education, the work of bringing equity into schools and classrooms invites consideration of what can be controlled and what cannot. Identifying and leveraging influence in small ways can make a difference in how equity is achieved or whether it is achieved at all.

I invite consideration of equity perhaps in ways not traditionally considered. With the addition of a nationwide survey, I have called upon educators to explore their vision of equity and to share how they have worked to make it a reality in their schools and classrooms.

Revisiting history will reveal that we have been here before. Doing so will help us clarify the need to move beyond the past and to use what we have learned to find more equitable educational opportunities going forward.

It is helpful to unpack the following questions:

- What is equity?
- What is equality?
- What can we control?
- What does equity look like in those places we have control?
- How can we achieve it?
- How can taking steps to implement it by creating a culture of justice foster greater understanding of ourselves and of one another?

Author's Note

As a public-school teacher and administrator coming from a public school "family business," I have long understood the importance of having a voice and truly listening to the voices of others. I was fortunate to have parents who supported and encouraged this in my upbringing, so transferring those beliefs and skills to my practice was somewhat second nature. Thus, my earliest and most significant learning experience with and about equity was that having a voice is an essential part of being recognized as one's unique self. There is a learning opportunity to share here: helping children find their voice is one aspect of equity.

I will never forget the time when, as a high school sophomore, during the planning for a religious school confirmation ceremony, I felt an injustice was being done when a parent tried to exert influence inappropriately over the process. My dad suggested I call the parent, listen to her perspective, and express my concerns to her. Hearing the hesitation in my voice, he said not to worry, that he would be on the line with me during the conversation—those were the days before cell phones!

So I made the call. Midway into our conversation, I heard a click. As I was still speaking with the parent, it became clear that the click was my dad hanging up on his end. After my conversation with the parent ended, successfully, I might add, I asked my dad why he had hung up. "You didn't need me," he said. "You were doing just fine on your own." This is yet another learning opportunity that I share: expressing confidence in children's abilities affords equity.

Unfortunately, not everyone has or has had the privilege of growing up the way I did. My mom, an upper elementary school teacher throughout much of her career, carried her parenting style into her classroom. One of the things I will never forget is how she believed students should be responsible for making decisions regarding their own behavior and also for sharing in the creation of a classroom culture of respect and fairness. She realized that if a child does not experience equity in their home, teachers can provide it in their classrooms—another learning experience to impart.

She set up a class court with opportunities for students to take part in "starring" roles: judge, jury, plaintiffs, and defendants. Whenever an issue came up potentially threatening the learning of one or more in the class, the court was in session! And it worked. Not that my mom was one of those teachers who banished students "to the office" for misbehavior. She wasn't. Not ever.

But holding court in her classroom created the opportunity for students to make decisions about how they interacted with others—and set an expectation for establishing relationships based on justice and fairness. She created equity in her classroom by giving students a voice, by inspiring the confidence of others in their classmates' abilities, and by making space for constructive experiences.

Mom taught in an urban suburb of Newark, New Jersey, during and after the Civil Rights Movement. Teaching fifth and sixth graders in an elementary school as she did was normally not an easy task—for that matter, teaching the oldest students in any school setting is never easy! But the race riots of the 1960s and the tempestuous years immediately following did not make her job any easier. Her compassionate approach to others and the creativity she brought to learning were never forgotten by her students.

On her passing in 2008, a student wrote that Mrs. Knobler had been his teacher at Chancellor Avenue School in Irvington many years ago. He remembered one thing. All the kids loved her. They undoubtedly loved the culture of justice and fairness she developed in the classroom and the equity-inspired confidence they acquired as well.

I share these stories by way of introduction to the pages that follow. History ebbs and flows—and many times that ebb and flow develop into seemingly unnavigable rapids. It is easy to get swept away. After my brief, but somewhat terrifying experience braving the rapids in Glacier National Park, I'm convinced the key to surviving is having a plan and executing it with the help of others. That is how I wrote this book.

I am dedicated to public education and the law and grateful to have grown up professionally during a time when the courts rendered many important decisions directly impacting education. Those affiliated with public school education are affected by those decisions and must plan according to the dictates of the courts. The passion educators bring to their practice every day—especially in times of seemingly overwhelming odds—only makes me more convinced of the power they hold and their potential to make the biggest difference in the lives of children.

Upon early retirement, I attended law school, which helped me return to my teaching roots as an adjunct professor of school law. I learn more every day about what motivates justices to make the decisions they make—knowledge that continues to expand and that helps me appreciate the importance of equity in schools and classrooms.

Common law, which is determined by the courts, is often limited in its reach. In part because of that, teachers and all those working with children, as well as the children themselves, are most influential in creating a culture of justice within which students may experience equity. It is my hope that my work here elicits that knowledge and supports the creative and untiring efforts of educators striving to create cultures in their classrooms respectful and caring to all.

It is difficult to move forward without recognizing our potential, and to recognize our potential, we need to understand the past. That understanding will help us all build better learning environments and opportunities together.

I must confess I was initially challenged about the approach to take in my research. So much is being written about equity in schools; so many "canned" programs for "social and emotional learning" (SEL), which is rapidly becoming a tired buzzword; so many theories and articles that have us chasing our tails. One thought was to just jump in—but the more I read and researched, the more webinars I attended, the more I realized that jumping in would only take me to an abyss—to a place where my own voice would be lost in the echoes of conclusions and quick fixes.

I considered incorporating learning theory with my work but decided to leave theory in the halls of academia. I considered looking at the history of education, but hearing about schooling to meet the needs of the industrial age was a poor fit for my objectives. I considered writing about the history of education, but there are so many histories out there with so many rabbit holes to explore….

I realized that to produce a truly useful and fresh understanding of equity meant that I needed to learn about people and to explore the things all people share despite the uniqueness of each person's experiences. I wanted to delve into what people feel, how they think, and how they respond to the world around them. To do this, I engaged in widely varied and rich reading and experiences of all sorts, getting to know people in the process. I was even fortunate to meet those with personal connections to court decisions and to hear and appreciate their stories firsthand.

An important part of my research was, and continues to be, reaching out to teachers and others intimately involved with public education—to all of you. My aim has been to find out what you believe equity and equality are and how (and if) they are different. I also sought to find out what you do in your schools to bring about equity for the kiddos with whom you interact—not from mass-produced prescriptions of publishing companies but from your own creative energy and inner strength that engages your agency in the classroom and enables you to foster agency in your students. What I discovered can be found in this book.

This book, then, is the story of my journey, the results of which I am eager to share. I hope what is revealed in these pages will afford you valuable connections to history, to the law, and to one another. I began this project envisioning my destination as a sharing of inspirational ways to best provide equity in public education. I hope we will reach that destination together as I truly believe the best inspiration comes from you.

Prologue

"Go to the masses. Don't write something that will just sit on the library shelves."

—Clint Smith[1]

That is exactly what I planned.

My family's summer-long cross-country adventures in the car were a perfect context for fights with my brother as to who would get the "bigger half" of the back seat! Of course, the "bigger half" is the perfect oxymoron in that it puts together two words that elicit very opposite images. Halves are equal so neither can be larger than the other. Yet, when it comes to determining fairness and justice, the division of a whole into two equal parts can be much more subtle, venturing into equity's domain.

Although anyone who works in the field of education is familiar with the words "equity" and "equality," people often mistake one term for the other or use them interchangeably. This confusion could result from the locus of control associated with each term and an understanding of when each best applies. For a long time, the terms were synonymous. How were educators to know the difference?

Equality is often associated in a one-dimensional sense with resource allocation but, on a more sophisticated and intangible level, with spheres of influence. Equality either exists or doesn't—and, in education, control over equality, more often than not, is considered in the distribution of consumables rather than in the assignment of authority.

In contrast, there is less of a bright line associated with equity because of the extraordinary range of very human variables upon which it rests. It is associated with justice and fairness, both of which are so dependent upon the observer's background and perspective, more likely to be imperceptible and less apt to be influenced by external factors.

So I decided to write this book to help us sort through the confusion. The real path to creating equity and the kind of equality that can be controlled by teachers and school leaders cuts through the red tape and the filing of reports. To address this topic in a meaningful and useful manner, I seek to distinguish between equity and equality, grounding their distinction in a study of the law presented as the stories of real people rather than dismissively as court edicts.

This is not a book that I wish to have sitting on your bookshelf. My intent is for this work to serve as a valuable resource, catching your attention, engaging your thinking, and motivating you to act.

Achieving equity and equality in education belongs not to the courts but to those on the front lines. It belongs to the people involved in the everyday operation of the schools—the teachers, foremost, but also many others working closely with students such as paraprofessionals, administrators, and, of course, the students themselves. These are the people who have the real power to make things happen—although they may not always realize this or have confidence in their ability to do so.

Perhaps the best support for this idea comes from an article written on the 50th Anniversary of the Supreme Court decision in *Brown v. Board of Education of Topeka*. In *The New Yorker* on May 3, 2004, Cass R. Sunstein wrote, "Before the Warren Court [which began in 1954], the justices were almost never a force for social reform…. Most of the time, the judiciary has been an obstacle to racial equality."[2]

Sunstein goes on to quote New York University Law Professor Larry D. Kramer who argues for "popular control over constitutional meaning," saying "The Supreme Court is not the highest authority in the land on constitutional law…. We are."[3] This is not to say that educators have the authority to overrule case law. It does strongly suggest, however, that educators, from their unique and special perspective on learning, must speak up for constitutional protections and work within the law to ensure these protections are in places where they *do* have control.

I invite you to come with me on a journey through the pages of what I hope is an enjoyable, thoughtful, and enlightening read. My goal is to share the history of equity and equality in the legal context of our American system of public education, using what we have learned from the past to help assure schooling focused on fairness and justice.

This book is designed to encourage reflection, build confidence, and develop a commitment to what is possible and "doable" more than it is a "how-to" book. I will share examples from the legal journey to equality in education that have helped set the stage for equity to even be possible. These examples come from my research. My work is complemented by what educators like you have shared.

The ideas in this book are, thus, a starting point. They have the potential to serve as a living resource, inspiring equity in public education. I hope you will make these pages live for the lives you touch in the noble work you do!

Some additional information and a few suggestions as you begin:

- Throughout the book, you will see open-ended questions designed to expand your thinking and elicit multiple possible responses. I pose these as a means of making my research and ideas more useful and more personal to your experiences, including the experiences you have with *your* students.

- Some questions are posed as "what-ifs." Many times, the slightest change in history can have a tremendous impact on everything that follows. This thinking is famously based on the "butterfly effect" theory of meteorologist Edward Lorenz "that a butterfly flapping its wings in Brazil could set off a tornado in Texas."[4]

Taking this metaphor to education, I interpret the flap of a butterfly's wings as the efforts of a teacher, administrator, support staff, paraprofessional, or student to effect equity in school. Using this metaphor, as a single butterfly's influence can impact a student or a classroom of students, imagine what the butterflies of a school or entire school system can do if they decide to create a culture of justice in education!

- As you read, also look for reflection questions that help you examine your own practice and/or what might be possible!

- The legal chapters *Equity? Who Says?*; *A Tale of Two Cases*; *Consequential, Unreliable, and Unpredictable*; and *Some Say Equity* are the "heart of the matter." Do not let yourself be put off by the language. The accounts shared are very much foundational to our understanding of why equity and equality have been so challenging in our public education system. You will uncover meaning and insight as you see the push and pull of attitudes progress through the cases. The stories in each case, taken separately and together, are compelling.

- Equity and equality are, as previously noted, terms that may seem interchangeable. I believe this is because they easily can be. Much of how these concepts are viewed depends upon one's frame of reference and priorities. Some may place greater weight on achieving equity; others on achieving equality. Neither is right or wrong. What is key is understanding from where each perspective is derived. I'm not convinced that even the courts have figured that out!

So, in retrospect, did my brother and I fight for equity in our back-seat car rides, or did we seek equality? A resolution based on equality could have been determined based on our ages, our size, our physical needs, or some other qualifier. The use of a ruler to determine seat share was sometimes threatened! A resolution based on equity could have considered the same factors as those for equality but with a focus on justice and fairness and, perhaps also, proportional sharing, consideration of each of our unique in-car activities and accompanying space needs, and even (as was often the case on our family trips) where bags would be stored that didn't quite fit into the trunk!

Chapter 1
The Black Panthers Meet the
Velveteen Rabbit

Black poet Langston Hughes speaks out in his poignant, *I, Too, Sing America,* of finally getting a seat at the table instead of being relegated to the kitchen as "the darker brother."[5] This is one way of looking at equity. There are so many interpretations of equity, of this idea—each very personal; each unique. No wonder it is so often misunderstood! No definition can adequately express its meaning or its promise.

One interpretation of equity comes from what may be a surprising source, the Black Panthers. In a loosely paraphrased "Ten-Point Program" of the Black Panther Party, Reynolds and Kendi use the term "real" to describe the Party's view of education.[6] The historical context of this Program speaks directly to the fight for racial justice in the 1960s with its words "We want education that teaches us our true history and our role in the present-day society."[7] This message resonates across time and equity, especially as education must be "real" for those receiving it. What this word implies is powerful in its simplicity, in its malleability, and in its potential.

So I ask:

- When you think of equity, equality, and schools, what is a "real education"?
- Is the term "real education" adequate to define equity or equality?
- Is "real" education more than what the courts say when they talk about a basic, minimal education?
- Does providing students with accurate and timely texts, adequate learning space in constructively healthy and secure facilities, sufficient

staff and resources, and opportunities embracing a full range of disciplines assure real education?

- Is that enough to make children independent?[8]
- By Langston Hughes' standard, does receiving a "real education" mean that all are welcomed to sit at the same table at the same time?

When I think of "real," the first thing that comes to my mind is the wonderful childhood story of *The Velveteen Rabbit.* Before banishing this connection as trivial, I urge you to think about its metaphorical potential. When the boy, so the story goes (who, never having been given a name, represents the "everychild"), was just a boy, his stuffed rabbit was real to him because he loved it. When he grew up, the idea of "real" took on added dimension when the nursery magic Fairy intervened to make the Velveteen Rabbit real to everyone.

The Skin Horse in the book explained that becoming real happens over time, when "most of your hair has been loved off, and your eyes drop out and you get loose in the joints and very shabby.... [I]t doesn't often happen to people who break easily, or have sharp edges...."[9]

Can we take a message from this that real education takes place when individuals are passionate about learning, and real education for everyone, collectively, takes time and effort to develop, demanding persistence, resilience, and flexibility? Or is that too much of a stretch? I think not, especially when conceptualizing equity as part of the foundation of a real education.

Isn't our goal as educators to provide for students something that is genuine and authentic, something that exists in fact? While the dictionary definitions of "real" and "equity" are not the same, one invokes the other as the concepts of genuineness and authenticity speak to justice and fairness, to an individual's truth. I would, therefore, interpret "real education" to mean opportunities that address each individual's essence and unique needs.

Unfortunately, though, as with a long history of court decisions assuring, but never quite delivering, a basic minimum education to all, identifying what is "real" very often gets in the way of the severity of reality itself. Knowing and addressing the reasons why the "darker brother" is sent to eat in the kitchen apart from the company are crucial to acknowledging the need for equity. The need for more specific direction in getting to that goal is elusive or missing when considering the simplicity and generosity of how education can be made "real."

I have many questions when I try to wrap my mind around the challenge of defining equity in a way that is palpable and achievable. For example:

- Who determines what equity *is* in any given situation? We have all seen pictures of children striving to look over a tall fence and standing on various-sized boxes to be able to do so. Sometimes, the determination of what is needed is easy—to look over a fence, one must be of a certain height. The boxes compensate for the differences. However, what if what is to be seen is not as easily discerned as that which can be viewed over a fence?

- Whose standard determines equity? What is necessary to make something real for one is not always what is necessary for another. Success is relative to one's expectations, and those expectations are based upon so many things, not the least of which includes the expectations of one's family, culture, race, ethnicity, age, locale, and place in history.

- For whom is equity necessary? Is the need for equity something that can or should always be imposed from another's viewpoint, or is the individual the best judge? Upon what factors does such a determination depend?

- When is a state of equity reached?

- Is it quantifiable?

- Who is responsible for administering equity?

- How can it be guaranteed?

- Are there times when equality is more important than equity? Who decides? When? How much?

For me, the answers to these questions are not only conditional but contingent upon certain realities. First, it matters not whether you are a child in a nursery, someone fighting for a cause, or one just trying to get through each day. We are all human; and there are important traits, competencies, and needs we share that require adjustments and flexibility in the ways we are helped to live our best lives. Next, becoming what one strives to become requires something different for every one of us and gives each person an education along the way.

How can schooling, something common to every individual though experienced in different forms, get us to the point where education is real for all? Where everyone has a seat at the table? Sharyl Allen from the Montana Department of Public Instruction (at the time of this writing) speaks to this in the context of education reform and increasing student agency saying, "You have to have deep in your being the desire to demonstrate respect and genuine caring and appreciation for what each person can bring to the table in this world we call education."[10]

It may be that achieving equity is contingent upon such desire so that everyone, including the "darker brother," may find their gifts welcome at the table.

Chapter 2
Equity? Who Says?
The Influence of the Courts and Common Law—Part I

"School began to reveal itself…as a child's game that one could not win."
—James Baldwin[11]

Let's face it. Teachers are on the receiving end for everything—students, supplies, criticism, and, hopefully more than occasionally, thanks for a job well done! Being on the receiving end, though, often keeps people in the dark about how what they are given comes to them. And that can be frustrating, making one feel helpless and powerless to effect any change for improvement. I know. Like you, I've been there.

I can share an insight from a superintendent with whom I worked very closely when I was a principal, especially as we were housed in the same building. "Beth," she said (taking some license with my paraphrasing here—it's been quite a while!), "you may think you know about decisions that are made, but you can never really know until you sit in this chair." I can say from experience that, even then, one does not always truly know or have a hand in those decisions.

What I have learned regarding equity is that, through state or federal legislation and data reporting, it is an expectation often thrust upon teachers and building administrators in their respective roles. That doesn't always have to be the case or the only way to view equity, but we'll get to that later.

To best understand, we will start with what is recognized as equity by the highest *legal* authorities—the U.S. Constitution and the courts. Something to think about as we explore the law coming from the courts (known as "common law") and, later, other types of legislation that influence education, is this sage insight from Clint Smith: "The path toward justice is long and uncertain. It sometimes moves forward and sometimes winds its way back."[12] It is always important to think about the path we choose to take, what motivates us to travel in that direction, and how we will deal with challenges that may turn us around.

"Equity" is mentioned in the Constitution only twice. Article III, Section 2, talks about the kinds of cases federal judges are empowered to decide. The Constitution reads, "The judicial Power shall extend to all Cases, in Law and Equity, arising under the Constitution, the Laws of the United States, and Treaties made, or which shall be made, under their Authority...."[13] "Equity," as used here, refers to justice and is the closest the Constitution comes to actually saying that the courts must be impartial. It is used similarly in Amendment XI that limits federal courts from becoming involved in suits by citizens of one state against those of another state or country.

To use the term "equity" is to imply that one is *acting with fairness*. As a "judicial power," equity is the responsibility of the courts to provide when rightful solutions cannot be found under existing laws (including those established by statute or common law such as determined by contracts or prior court decisions, i.e., property law, personal injury law, etc.). Justices, thus, have the power to "do equity," by tailoring their judgment to the particular needs of a case. Equity is flexible, practical, and designed to recognize both the needs of the public and the private individual.

But how have the courts weighed in on equity as regards the *rights* of United States citizens? The word "equity" doesn't always appear in key court cases that have addressed this. Sometimes, what may be intended as "equity" is referred to in judicial opinions as "equality" (though the word "equality" is mentioned neither in the Constitution nor in its 27 amendments). The exchange of these two terms may be a simple issue of semantics, or it may be the justices' way of tempering their ruling, using one to indicate an inability or unwillingness to meet the standards of the other.

What follows are several significant court cases that have helped to set some parameters for schoolhouse equity. This list is far from complete; however, it does provide some important background and a glimpse into an ongoing struggle for justice.

- *Roberts v. City of Boston* (1849) is recognized as the earliest court case addressing school equity. It concerned the right of an African American child, Sarah Roberts, to attend a school designated for white children rather than the Abiel Smith School that served black children. The Abiel Smith School, in addition to being much farther from Sarah's home than several schools for white children, was also overcrowded and underfunded with inadequate facilities.

What prompted this case was the response of the Primary School Committee of the City of Boston to a challenge by black parents frustrated by the assignment of their children to what they believed were inferior schools. The Committee "argued that Black schoolchildren's 'peculiar physical, mental, and moral structure, requires an educational treatment, different, in some respects from that of white children.'"[14]

Noted abolitionist lawyer Charles Sumner was co-counsel representing five-year-old Sarah Roberts and her father. The Plaintiffs lost the case, but Sumner's prophetic argument that racial segregation of schools "'is a violation of equality'"[15] would set the stage for what was to come over the next century.

- Sumner's cautionary tale was that "'The separation of the schools, so far from being for the benefit of both races, is an injury to both. It tends to create a feeling of degradation in the blacks, and of prejudice and uncharitableness in the whites.'"[16] His words echoed in the Supreme Court's 1896 ruling in a case known as *Plessy v. Ferguson*, involving the plight of a black man who easily "passed" for white and who dared to take a seat in a train car reserved only for white people in violation of Louisiana's Separate Car Act requiring whites and blacks to occupy separate railway cars.

The court ruled against Homer Plessy, cementing the rule of "separate but equal" and legitimized differentiation of access by race to effectively everything society could offer, at least legally, until the *Brown* case in 1954 (see following). The *Plessy* decision emboldened the discriminatory Jim Crow laws in the South and added to tremendous disparities in the quality of education across the nation.[17]

There is a most interesting and very recent twist to this story. In November 2021, after more than a century, the Louisiana State Board of Pardons decided, unanimously, to clear Homer Plessy of the charges against him and to pass their decision along to Louisiana's governor for pardon under a state law known as the Avery C. Alexander Act, which allows for someone "…convicted of violating a state law or municipal ordinance the purpose of which was to maintain or enforce racial separation or discrimination of individuals, upon application to the Board of Pardons [to] be granted a pardon for the conviction."[18]

Speaking to the Board of Pardons in 2021, Jason Williams, Orleans Parish district attorney, said of the 1896 decision, "There is no doubt that he [Plessy] was guilty of that act on that date…. But there is equally no doubt that such an act should have never been a crime in this country."[19] Clearly, here is evidence of the unspeakable and vast impact of the law in our country's past. Actions clearing Homer Plessy also beg us to consider justice and the role of equity.

On January 5, 2022, Louisiana's Governor John Bel Edwards issued a posthumous pardon to Plessy saying he was "beyond grateful" for the opportunity to affirm Plessy's "legacy of the rightness of his cause…undefiled by the wrongness of his conviction."[20]

Other cases have come and gone, each making a dent in the quest for educational equity, though meeting up against odds difficult to surmount in their time.

- The story behind *Tape v. Hurley* (1885) was of American-born Mamie Tape, a child of Chinese heritage, whose parents sought to enroll her in the Spring Valley Primary School in San Francisco. California did pass a law in 1880 allowing all California residents to attend public schools, but the Chinese Exclusion Act in 1882 stood in the way of Chinese immigration and citizenship for a period of 10 years. Although the Superior Court Judge ruled in Mamie's favor that "all children, including immigrants, were entitled to public education," she never was admitted to Spring Valley Primary School on the basis of local school board policies and the social mores of the time that the then State Superintendent of Public Instruction worried would "throw open our public schools to the Chinese."[21]

- One of the first equity cases specifically regarding the *funding* of public schools was *Cumming v. Richmond County Board of Education* in 1899. Claiming economic hardship, the Richmond County Board of Education determined it would fund only the high school designated for white children, temporarily closing that designated for children of color, even though parents of the students in both schools paid taxes used to run those institutions.

- A case similar to both *Tape* and *Cumming* is that of *Gong Lum v. Rice* where the U.S. Supreme Court affirmed the decision of the Mississippi Supreme Court saying that Martha Lum, of Chinese ancestry but born in the United States, was to be denied admission to a high school exclusively for whites but to which her father paid taxes as a resident. This action was consistent with the Mississippi State Constitution that provided "Separate schools shall be maintained for children of the white and colored races."[22]

- Children of Mexican ancestry seeking equity were the 1931 plaintiffs in *Roberto Alvarez v. The Board of Trustees of the Lemon Grove School District*, where the Mexican-American children, after starting the 1930–1931 school year together with white students in Lemon Grove, found themselves returning in January 1931 relegated to a school built just for them nicknamed "'La Caballeriza' (the barnyard)."[23] Working through the Mexican Consulate, the parents of the Mexican-American children filed suit—and won—establishing "the rights of their children to equal education, despite local, regional and national sentiment that favored not only segregation, but the actual deportation of the Mexican population in the United States."[24]

Lemon Grove is a case not widely known perhaps because it never went further than the Superior Court of California. It actually was, however, a monumental decision in that it was the very first successful desegregation case in the United States—13 years before *Brown* (which we will look at soon).

- *Lemon Grove* was followed in 1946 by the ruling in *Mendez v. Westminster*, a complaint filed by parents of children excluded from certain schools on the basis of their "Mexican and Latin" ancestry. Comments credited to the defendants during the trial included one superintendent's references to Mexicans' inferior abilities, economic outlook, personal hygiene (specifically mentioning "lice, impetigo, tuberculosis, and generally dirty hands, neck, face and ears"), and deficiencies in English to the point that they could not learn Mother Goose rhymes.[25]

This argument recalls the thinking in *Roberts*, also seen in *Tape* and other cases, where justices and individuals especially influential in ensuring equitable education for all children relied on social mores and biases to shape their views about people who were different than they were.

Mendez brought together regional, racial, and ethnic groups that supported its efforts to overcome "systemic prejudice, confronting issues of race, class and citizenship."[26] Among the takeaways from *Mendez* was the passage in California of the Anderson Bill that effectively ended school segregation in that state—an important postscript to all of these stories that have a common theme of state constitutions controlling the provision of public school education. This bill was signed by the then-governor of California, Earl Warren, who would later write the Court's opinion in *Brown*. (Now, that's where we're going next!)

- The seminal case of *Brown v. Board of Education of Topeka* (known as *Brown I*) always comes to mind when thinking about equity and equality in education. Actually, a compilation of several similar cases from Kansas, South Carolina, Virginia, Delaware, and Washington, D.C., this case resulted in one of the Supreme Court's most well-known judgments, "[I]n the field of public education the doctrine of 'separate but equal' has no place. Separate but equal facilities are inherently unequal."[27]

This case was not the first example of Supreme Court intervention in public education, but it was, perhaps, the first time the Court examined the right to an education, something never determined as "fundamental" under the U.S. Constitution and always controlled independently by the states. Its impact is seen in the many subsequent cases where states struggled (and still do struggle) to effectively desegregate schools despite attempts after the Civil War and

Reconstruction that explicitly, or as a matter of consequence, defined where people of color were and were not allowed to live.

The need for equality in education is front and center in Chief Justice Warren's opinion in this case:

Today, education is perhaps the most important function of state and local governments. Compulsory school attendance laws and the great expenditures for education both demonstrate our recognition of the importance of education to our democratic society. It is required in the performance of our most basic public responsibilities, even service in the armed forces. It is the very foundation of good citizenship. Today it is a principal instrument in awakening the child to cultural values, in preparing him for later professional training, and in helping him to adjust normally to his environment. In these days, it is doubtful that any child may reasonably be expected to succeed in life if he is denied the opportunity of an education. Such an opportunity, where the state has undertaken to provide it, is a right which must be made available to all on equal terms. We come then to the question presented: does segregation of children in public schools solely on the basis of race, even though the physical facilities and other 'tangible' factors may be equal, deprive the children of the minority group of equal educational opportunities? We believe that it does.[28]

It is important to take note of the reasons Warren cites for the importance of education. These will be echoed in future cases, as well as throughout the rest of this study. They are essential to providing equity of educational opportunity for all children: the performance of basic public responsibilities, service in the armed forces, good citizenship, cultural values, preparation for later professional training, and help in adjusting normally to one's environment.

- Although the *Brown* court delivered a unanimous verdict in favor of school desegregation, sadly, this case became a powerful illustration that, while the highest court has the ability to rule, it lacks the actual authority to *implement* its ruling. In the year following its decision in *Brown*, the Supreme Court attempted to enforce this desegregation ruling. In a case that has been referred to as *Brown II*, the Court heard from states with segregated systems of education, including Florida,

North Carolina, Arkansas, Oklahoma, Maryland, and Texas. While the Court recognized progress toward desegregation made in some states, it noted continuing challenges facing school boards that required local agencies and states to address roadblocks along the way.

In his opinion in *Brown II*, Chief Justice Warren explains constitutional equity when he refers to the need for the lower courts in each of the *Brown I* cases to implement desegregation as "guided by equitable principles." These, he says, are "characterized by a practical flexibility in shaping remedies and a facility for adjusting and reconciling public and private needs."[29] Again, these are key words to hold in place as our story continues. We will put them to good use later!

A takeaway from *Brown II* is the Court's reaffirming the importance of desegregating schools "as soon as practicable on a nondiscriminatory basis" by eliminating "a variety of obstacles in making the transition to school systems operated in accordance with the constitutional principles" in *Brown I*.[30] That the Court often talks in vague terms like these leaves one scratching their head to figure out what has been said. For example, one would wonder what is the length of a timeline that is "as soon as practicable"? Indeed, this is what likely capsized *Brown's* effectiveness (though that was not the only challenge, as we'll see in later chapters). The Court explains it as a "prompt and reasonable start towards full compliance" with additional time as is "necessary to carry out the ruling in an effective manner" and "necessary to the public interest."[31]

What "variety of obstacles" does the Court envision districts as having to surmount in moving toward desegregating public schools? The Chief Justice explains those obstacles could include:

> *...the physical condition of the school plant, the school transportation system, personnel, revision of school districts and attendance areas into compact units to achieve a system of determining admission to the public schools on a nonracial basis, and revision of local laws and regulations which may be necessary in solving the foregoing problems.*[32]

Even though *Brown II* did not, in fact, have the push that *Brown I* had hoped for, it endeavored to lay more specific groundwork for the actual desegregation of public schools. In doing so, however, it also managed to set the course for oh-so-many legal challenges to desegregation that began almost immediately after it was decided.

- Although not a court case itself, the first challenge to hit the scene was *The Southern Manifesto*, which represented the position of 19 Senators in 11 states and 77 members of the House, also from a number of states.[33] This was presented to Congress in March 1956, only two years after the first *Brown* decision and one year following *Brown II*. It was the voice of Southern states and legislators committed to a litany of protections that, in their belief, were afforded by segregation. This call to action spurred more than five decades of pushback against *Brown*, with the latest case to go to the U.S. Supreme Court's being *Parents Involved in Community Schools v. Seattle School Dist. No. 1* in 2007.

The *Manifesto* argued that the federal government had overstepped its authority by determining, in *Brown*, that "separate but equal" has no place in public education. Their basis for this assertion was that the outright guarantee of a public education is nowhere to be found in the U.S. Constitution (true), appearing only as granted through the jurisdiction of the individual states known as "states' rights" under the 10th Amendment.

If that weren't bad enough, the *Manifesto* sent out a call to States and their citizens to consider whether they, themselves, had been victimized by the Court's involvement and praised States "resist[ing] forced integration by any lawful means."[34] Those penning the *Manifesto* added a final proviso appealing "to our people not to be provoked by the agitators and troublemakers invading our States and to scrupulously refrain from disorder and lawless acts,"[35] perhaps to give this document the respectability they felt might be needed to convince nonbelievers. History, both of the later twentieth century and of the most recent date, has shown that the appeal for a measured and civil response to integration fell on deaf ears.

- A number of cases have had to do with equity in school funding, but none has been so influential as *San Antonio v. Rodriguez* in 1973, which legitimized wealth inequity in the allocation of tax dollars to support public education. This lawsuit was brought by poor Texas citizens residing in communities lacking sufficient funding from their tax base to put their schools on par with those of wealthier districts across the state—despite additional state funding intended "to help offset disparities in local spending and to meet Texas' changing educational requirements."[36] In its discussion the Court compared the Plaintiff's community, a poor, predominantly Mexican-American population, with its polar opposite, a district with a wealthy, predominantly white population also located in proximity to San Antonio.

The opinion from the divided Court identified what Texas believes is an "adequate" education that includes "12 years of free public-school education, …teachers, books, transportation, and operating funds."[37] The opinion also noted that constitutional Equal Protection "does not require absolute equality or precisely equal advantages. Nor, indeed, in view of the infinite variables affecting the educational process, can any system assure equal quality of education except in the most relative sense."[38] The Court went on to say that the class of plaintiffs filing the suit was neither "saddled with such disabilities, or subjected to such a history of purposeful unequal treatment, or relegated to such a position of political powerlessness as to command extraordinary protection from the majoritarian political process."[39]

This was the Supreme Court's qualification of what would merit special consideration in education funding—and it did *not* include Rodriguez and the other Plaintiffs. Though, as has been said by other courts in the past and continuing into the present (and likely the future), the fact that education is not regarded as a "fundamental" right under the U.S. Constitution doesn't take away the ability to obtain protections ensuring financial equity for all students.

Other courts have tried, with some success, to achieve equity in funding their schools—though only at the state level and without the impact of the Supreme Court's lasting, unshakable impression in *Rodriguez*. A good example of how the courts still grapple with this issue of ensuring equity on the basis of wealth can be seen in the case of *Leandro v. State of North Carolina*, which actually began in 1994 and continues to the present day.

As in *Brown*, North Carolina's Supreme Court in *Leandro*, despite finding that every child is entitled to a "sound basic education." has encountered difficulty in ensuring that right. That court's determination of exactly what is meant by a "sound basic education" includes "Classrooms with competent, certified, well-trained teachers; Schools led by competent, well-trained principals; Resources necessary to support effective instructional programs."[40]

Of additional note is the most recent case (as of this writing) addressing equity in state school funding, *William Penn School District v. Pennsylvania Department of Education,* which, in February 2023, established that disparities existed among Pennsylvania districts on the basis of wealth, as determined by property values, that deny students equitable learning/schooling opportunities. The decision coming from the Commonwealth Court requires that those in government and administrative agencies responsible for education devise a plan addressing "constitutional deficiencies" in recognition of the reality that "in the 21st century, students need more than a desk, chair, pen, paper, and textbooks." From the court order, citing the Pennsylvania Constitution Education Clause, Article III, Section 14, "every student [is required to] receive a meaningful opportunity to succeed academically, socially, and civically, which requires that all students have access to a comprehensive, effective, and contemporary system of public education."[41]

- One of the more famous, and some might argue, successful examples of a state funding challenge to equalize opportunities according to wealth is the New Jersey case of *Abbott v. Burke.* This state funding challenge to equalize opportunities in districts serving poor populations, largely people of color, began in 1981 and continues to this very day.[42]

New Jersey school districts are classified according to a rather complex demographic formula that identifies them in a range from "A" through "J": "A" districts are essentially the poorest; "J" districts are the wealthiest. Put very simply, funding derived on the basis of the *Abbott* litigation provides state money to supplement the local tax share for education in the "A" districts, bringing them to the funding levels of the "J" districts "[t]o ensure the children in these schools a 'thorough and efficient' education, as required by the New Jersey Constitution."[43]

As with any endowment or fund allocation, there is not only a mountain of paperwork but also many strings attached where the State or another funding source dictates exactly how those monies are to be spent. In this regard, the relative authority of school administrators and school boards can be vastly different between the "A" and "J" districts—especially as the coffers of the State's wealthiest districts are often supplemented by independent community-funded education foundations supporting local education initiatives for districts and individual teachers.

This list of cases could go on and on, but there is one additional set of related cases that is noteworthy because it brings together the past and the immediate present as well as concerns about funding and program equity. What follows is helpful as an introduction.

The 1970s marked the end of the "Great Migration," a period of time that began around 1910 when African Americans, slaves and descendants of former slaves, left the South for what they felt would be more accepting societies west and north. Their migration completely changed the racial and social dynamic of some of our largest cities, perhaps none more than Detroit. With the influx of people of color, a phenomenon that became known as "white flight" took place. Isabel Wilkerson describes this as "a fitful migration of whites out of their urban strongholds…seeking, with government incentives, to replicate the havens they once had in the cities."[44]

To give you an idea of how quickly that happened in Detroit, around the time of World War I, the black population of Detroit grew from 5,741 to 41,000[45] and "from 1.4 percent to 44 percent during the era of the [Great] Migration."[46] That demographic continues to the current day with black and African American residents making up 82% of Detroit's population.[47]

Additionally, there have been what may be referred to as "micro-migrations" where urban planning has either displaced those living in established black communities or imposed covenants in the development of neighborhoods for the purpose of excluding people on the basis of race or religion. Although these covenants may no longer be legally enforced, they continue to impact neighborhoods such as those divided by Troost Avenue in Kansas City, Missouri. Vestiges of these so-called improvements remain today, highly visible in the effect they have had on schools, an illustration being the 1990 Supreme court decision in *Missouri v. Jenkins* that focused on the Kansas City schools. I mention urban planning here to point out its significant connection to education equity. It is important to bear in mind the dangers inherent in oversimplification, however, as the purpose of this book is not to detail the intricacies of neighborhood development but to speak to the history and realities of achieving equity in public schools. While one factor may predominate, many contribute to changes in communities.[48]

To return to Detroit:

- *Milliken v. Bradley*, a case centering on Detroit decided in 1974, was one of many challenges to the constitutionality of desegregation after *Brown. Bradley* was less of a challenge based on a distribution of wealth to achieve equity and more an effort to "establish a unitary nonracial school system" incorporating the city of Detroit and the "85 outlying school districts... [in] three counties."[49]

Recalling the prophetic concerns of Chief Justice Warren in *Brown II* about being able to revise district sending units to assure attendance on a nonracial basis, the ruling in this case allowed the city of Detroit to remain separate from its surrounding suburbs. In effect, *Bradley* normalized and justified racial imbalance brought on as a result of, among other things, white flight and redlining that minimized opportunities for people of color to have their children attend suburban schools.[50]

- The impact of *Bradley* became more about wealth in a recent case also concerning the Detroit public schools, *Gary B. v. Whitmer*. Plaintiffs, students from the lowest performing public schools in Detroit, alleged that their inadequate performance was due to "poor conditions within their classrooms, including missing or unqualified teachers, physically dangerous facilities, and inadequate books and materials...depriv[ing] them of a basic minimum education...provid[ing] a chance at foundational literacy."[51] According to the Plaintiffs, this situation has worsened since the 1990s when the State took over the Detroit schools both in response to "'fiscal deficit and failing student achievement outcomes.'"[52]

The Sixth Circuit, in its analysis in *Gary B.*, can be seen referring to the topic of our study when it says, "'[T]hat education is a means of achieving equality in our society' is a belief 'that has persisted in this country since the days of Thomas Jefferson'"[53] and in its conclusion, that "Education has long been viewed as a great equalizer, giving all children a chance to meet or outperform society's expectations, even when faced with substantial disparities in wealth and with past and on-going racial inequality."[54] Looking at what Plaintiffs cite as wealth disparities and evidence of inequity, we see a list remarkably similar to that in *Leandro*: the quality of teacher preparation, materials, and building conditions not suitable for learning.

What power this gives to those of us in education to make a difference! Education as "a great equalizer"!

I wish I could report that *Gary B.* actually continued to the U.S. Supreme Court where another issue it raised about education as a fundamental right could again be debated. Unfortunately, the case stopped at the Sixth Circuit with Governor Whitmer's agreeing to provide funding to address issues Plaintiffs raise as shortfalls. Whether this funding will make a difference or whether the concerns brought in *Gary B.,* as with *Leandro* and *Abbott,* will drag on indefinitely with no clear resolution remains to be seen. In this case, at least, the opportunity for continued support for the students in Detroit from the courts has stopped as a condition of the agreement to provide additional funding for the schools. The case will go no further.

I could go on with other similar examples of continuing litigation aimed at desegregating schools and equalizing funding and resources (both human and material), especially in urban schools. Based upon this short analysis of court history, it appears that common law views education equity and equality as contingent on both the allocation of tax dollars and a belief that people are people, no matter their race, ethnicity, or religion. Mind you, this view is anything but a clear picture, rather one that goes in and out of focus, and, like a spotty Internet connection, can be relied upon as a source of frustration when it freezes or shuts people out altogether. To reiterate the words that began this chapter from Clint Smith, "The path toward justice is long and uncertain."

What does all this mean for educators? From the perspective of common law, what is within our control and what is not?

Funding

Not in our control:

- Allocations of federal, state, and local tax funding can best be influenced by electing those who support equity in education and relying on them to represent students' best interests.

Potentially within our control:

- Recommendations for spending within schools and districts—including suggestions from staff to administration for resources to improve equitable opportunities for all students.
- Advocacy from administrators during the budgetary process for staffing and resources. This will vary from district to district and state to state in terms of the amount and type of authority and autonomy teachers and administrators have in the budgetary process. However, advocacy can take a variety of forms including:
  - Applying for grants (both within and beyond district walls)
  - Sourcing educational foundation monies
  - Campaigning for the creation of such foundations
  - Partnering with local businesses and industry for financial as well as human resources (which could include items such as cast-off furniture from company remodels)
  - Submitting proposals to the district administration for opportunities to engage students and staff with the community including apprenticeships and programs extending the school day and year

Desegregation

Not in our direct control as educators except, as with funding, by using our voices as voters.

Potentially within our control:

- Advocacy by raising a voice in the community for changes to zoning and alternative approaches to the delivery of schooling that engage schools in the community
- Serving as a community-to-community ambassador to build bridges between people, including students, staff, and parents
- Partnering for programs and progress to break down barriers and challenge stereotypical thinking
- Courageously speaking out against discrimination of any form in schools where one has influence

- Using instructional materials that speak to humanity, generate understanding through the sharing of truths, and prompt students to engage in critical thinking

Chapter 3
Equity? Who Says?
The Influence of the Courts and Common Law—Part II

A Tale of Two (or So) Cases

"It was the best of times, it was the worst of times…it was the spring of hope, it was the winter of despair…."

—Charles Dickens[55]

- 1859—the year that Charles Dickens wrote *A Tale of Two Cities*.
- 1859—only several years after the very first legal challenge to racially-separate schools in the United States—schools in the heart of Boston, not the deep South.

Dickens' words resonate in the context of legal decisions then and into the present day—decisions that have bounced public education between optimism and anguish, from words of wisdom to postulations that, especially in hindsight, may only be viewed as reckless. Yet this is the legacy of our courts, especially of our highest court. One can take those decisions with a reasonable amount of skepticism and a modicum of trust as to the true impact the justices' deliberations have had on schools—or one can run with them as a roadmap to understanding history. Or both.

It is very hard to resist the temptation to ask "what if" when legal challenges are cast and courts rule. There is no question that the what-ifs are worth pondering—including how legal challenges have determined the course of time, intentionally or as unintended consequences of justices' sensibilities.

Am I suggesting that personal biases influence jurisprudence? Yes, inevitably. Nowhere in the Constitution, including in its 27 amendments, is there the promise of impartiality among justices. Justices are under the influence of history and society—inconsistencies in their decisions reflect the shifting composition of the courts and the times. To quote Soren Kierkegaard, "Life can only be understood backwards; but it must be lived forwards."[56]

Thus, as we take what we can from the courts, running with the victories and challenging the setbacks, it is important to realize the fragility of justice and the potential for its echo through time. Like an echo, some decisions hit hard with a case or cases that follow where clear and consistent facts allow justices to apply one answer to different challenges. In other cases, though, where the outline of a challenge is not as clear, just as an echo hits a soft surface and is absorbed, so the decision of the court can fail to resonate with the new challenge. The echo of the decision fades as it is either overturned or becomes obsolete.

It is a valuable exercise, therefore, for those potentially affected by a court decision, particularly a decision of the U.S. Supreme Court, to find out how the justices have ruled and to consider how that ruling may impact them. One way to do the latter is to explore the "what-ifs." Doing so affords consideration of a decision from several points of view.

The what ifs of two momentous Supreme Court decisions stand out with regard to education: the cases of *Plessy v. Ferguson* and *Brown I*. I almost want to call these decisions "watershed" cases. However, it is important to understand that a watershed event is one after which nothing is ever the same. Recent Supreme Court rulings have been displaying or hinting at new attitudes toward the precedent-setting decisions of the past. More than ever before, we are now seeing that no decision can be taken for granted as absolute. This can work to the advantage or to the disadvantage of public education, particularly when it comes to honoring each person as an individual.

Plessy was that seminal case that legalized "separate but equal," cementing what *Roberts v. City of Boston* had started almost 50 years earlier and legitimizing Jim Crow injustices for 50 years to come. I always tell my law students that even though a case isn't directly involved with education, one can never predict its reach. So it is with *Plessy*.

What if Plessy had won? We know that Plessy has been pardoned posthumously by Louisiana's governor. But what if he had originally been found innocent in 1892 when he was first brought to trial? Or when his case went to the Supreme Court in 1896?

What some may not know is that Plessy's arrest was a bit of a setup in the first place to challenge what, from one perspective, was viewed as a discriminatory railroad practice and something the railroad wanted to see changed because of the additional costs it incurred in having to purchase and run both "white" and "colored" cars. This would explain how authorities knew that Plessy, who was seven-eighths white and one-eighth black, was actually of mixed race—they were in on it from the start! In fact, both Plessy's actions of taking a seat in the "white" train car, as well as his arrest, were carefully orchestrated.[57] Even with a careful strategy in place, though, this legal challenge to Louisiana's Separate Car Act was a gamble. So why invest time, money, and energy?

I also always tell my students that an issue doesn't become an issue unless someone challenges it. Even with the risk of losing, the dedication of many to treating people justly and fairly is always worth the battle. It was no different in the 1890s. Putting Homer Plessy on that train forced the highest court to commit to either a segregated society or one that treated people as people.

It is not that the effort to achieve integration on the trains was legally flawed. Quite to the contrary. Plessy's legal team was a group of legacy lawyers with impressive pedigrees and political connections. Nor was this case merely a provincial issue focused on one law in one state. This case cast a wide net, its genesis extending all the way to the north in Massachusetts where the same ticket was *supposed to* secure seats wherever the patrons wished to sit.

The reality, even in the North, was much the opposite with the preferable "white" cars reserved only for white patrons and seats on the less-than-desirable "colored" cars reserved only for black patrons. Despite promises of open seating coming from those funding the Massachusetts railroad expansion and a Massachusetts state Constitution that guaranteed equal treatment, all bets were off once fares were paid. Even Frederick Douglass, a free black man, was thrown off a white car along with other protestors while riding the train in Massachusetts.[58]

So what if Homer Plessy's defense team *had* won? What if the U.S. Supreme Court had abolished "separate but equal" on train cars in the late 1800s? Would that ruling have extended to all aspects of life, perhaps even thwarting attempts to impose Jim Crow laws across the South? Would such efforts have impacted schools to the extent that there would have been no need for the cases involved in the *Brown* decision to ever have come to the Court?

My guess is a firm no. Justices have shown us with their words, and a society of people have shown us by their actions, that despite judicial decree, it would be virtually impossible to monitor every breach or to challenge every practice reflecting ingrained societal beliefs. A ruling on segregation by the Fourth Circuit in the early 1950s gives great perspective. District Judge Bryan in that case (which later became part of *Brown I*) said in his opinion.

It indisputably appears from the evidence that the separation provision rests neither upon prejudice, nor caprice, nor upon any other measureless foundation. Rather the proof is that it declares one of the ways of life in Virginia. Separation of white and colored 'children' in the public schools of Virginia has for generations been a part of the mores of her people. To have separate schools has been their use and wont.[59]

Yet the Judge also conceded that conditions in the "Negro schools" were vastly different from those in white schools, noting, in particular, the buildings and facilities provided for learning, student transportation, and curricula.[60]

A perfect example of the disconnect between the beliefs and actions of those sitting on the bench comes from another case—not an education case but one also with a clear lesson for schools. It was a challenge during World War II by Fred Korematsu, a man who refused orders to leave home and report to a relocation center along with other Japanese Americans. After the attack on Pearl Harbor, fear of those of Japanese heritage was so great that the United States took action that at the time, the country felt was necessary to protect Americans from enemies abroad. The problem, of course, was that in doing this, the United States essentially established its own detention camps singling out a population of citizens on the basis of race for life-altering emotional, mental, and physical abuse.

Justice Hugo Black (a former member of the Ku Klux Klan who had resigned from the organization a number of years prior to this case[61]) wrote the court's opinion. Robert Chang, the Founder and Executive Director of the Fred T. Korematsu Center for Law and Equality, in an unpublished op-ed piece shared on Twitter, quotes Justice Black as having said:

'All legal restrictions which curtail the civil rights of a single racial group are immediately suspect' and that 'racial antagonism never can justify such curtailment.' Powerful words. But Black found no racial animus, even though other (white) ethnic/national origin groups, whose countries were at war against the U.S., were not subjected to anything like what happened to 120,000 persons of Japanese ancestry.[62]

Although Korematsu initially lost in 1944, in a move that would later be echoed in Homer Plessy's 2022 posthumous pardon, Chief Justice Roberts, in his 2018 opinion in *Trump v. Hawaii*, said, "*Korematsu* was gravely wrong the day it was decided, has been overruled in the court of history, and—to be clear—'has no place in law under the Constitution.'"[63] However, while *Plessy* was reversed by the Supreme Court in 1954 with *Brown I*, Korematsu was never similarly vindicated. The year 1983 did bring a small victory when his conviction was cleared by the U.S. District Court of Northern California in San Francisco.

The impact here on education is severalfold. First, it is good to understand that those in positions of influence will not always perceive the world in a way that is logical or fair. Skepticism is sometimes the best response when legal opinions appear to use bias and distort justice. Next, sometimes, it is a good idea to spark a challenge when things appear to be unjust. Both Homer Plessy and Fred Korematsu were test cases for perceived injustices. Students need to know how important it is for them to think critically about their world and ways to approach injustice honorably and civilly using their constitutional rights. And, finally, know that things that may appear to be the "worst of times" can sometimes deliver what may lead to "the best of times." *Brown* will take us there, at least with good intentions.

When the Warren Court first took on the several desegregation cases that were joined for what eventually became the decision in *Brown I*, the Chief Justice at that time, Fred Vinson, opposed integration. The justices of the Vinson Court were much divided with their opinions ranging from maintaining *Plessy's* "separate but equal" ruling to outright ending it, to taking a "wait and see" approach based on concerns of Southern violence.[64]

When the Chief Justice became frustrated at failing to bring the Court together, Justice Felix Frankfurter proposed that the Court hear a second round of arguments with each of the parties given certain questions to which they would respond. Life happens in funny ways sometimes. Just prior to this second round of arguments, Chief Justice Vinson had a heart attack and died. He was succeeded by Earl Warren, who delivered a unanimous decision by the Court saying in his opinion that:

Segregation of white and colored children in public schools has a detrimental effect upon the colored children. The impact is greater when it has the sanction of the law, for the policy of separating the races is usually interpreted as denoting the inferiority of the negro group.... We conclude that, in the field of public education, the doctrine of 'separate but equal' has no place. Separate educational facilities are inherently unequal.[65]

To address the concerns of unrest in the South after this decision was rendered, the Court determined not to immediately end segregation as was the request of Thurgood Marshall and the NAACP who had argued on behalf of the Plaintiffs. The Court decided to solicit proposals for timelines and strategies to end segregation from those states favoring it.[66]

I said that *Brown* would take us to the "best of times" at least with good intentions; however, the push and pull of various committees set up in the southern states and at the University of North Carolina during and immediately after the ruling revealed deep-seated biases and attitudes that were unconvinced and unchanged by the opinion of the Court. To fully understand the impact of *Brown* is to see it as the sister decision to *Plessy*, which is revealing as to why these two partner cases are the primary focus of this chapter.

Brown, I was a sweeping, wide-ranging ruling. It was a case about the extent of an entitlement to public education that overturned a decision (in *Plessy*) about society as a whole. Powerful! At the same time, as Chief Justice Warren was speaking of education as "perhaps the most important function of state and local governments" and "the importance of education to our democratic society,"[67] conversations, indeed arguments, were had as to how far the reach of this decision would go.

One of those "conversations" was actually the first segregation lawsuit. Filed with the Fourth Circuit in June 1955, it pitted three black students against the oldest public university in the United States, the University of North Carolina. The University had a strict policy against admitting black students as undergrads, allowing them admission only as graduate students into those programs of study unavailable at the "Negro schools."[68] The issue, in this case, was whether the decision in *Brown I* applied only to K-12 public schools or, also, to public universities with the Defendants' perspective being that "separate but equal" had been settled with *Plessy* and that in *Brown I,* the Court had overstepped its authority.

This was not the only case against a public university, another having been filed in February 1956 against the University of Alabama. In many ways, the challenges to *Brown I* from the universities were a clear message that they chose to operate as though *Plessy* was still the law.

What happened as a result of these challenges? The three Plaintiffs eventually were admitted to the University of North Carolina, starting their academic year quite a bit after their white colleagues—even after the University's attempted appeal, which an editorial in the *Daily Tar Heel* called a "Ridiculous Anti-Climax." The editorial accused the University Trustees of a "needless, unjustified, and prejudiced attack" and noted how well the black students had been received by the majority. The editorial downplayed concerns that desegregation "would bring discord" to campus, heralding the court's decision as quite to the contrary.[69]

Not to be defeated, after being ordered by a federal court to admit black students, the University determined that it would change the standards by which students would be admitted. Applicants would now be required to score in the top three quartiles on three separate tests. This change instantly disadvantaged black students who, by virtue of their race, had been educated at schools far inferior to those white students had attended. As Geeta Kapur notes in *To Drink from the Well*, the University "obeyed the letter of the law but not its spirit."[70]

Stories from post-*Brown* history reveal that *Brown I*, decided in May 1954, truly was the "'spring' of hope" in Dickens' words, which led to the "'winter' of despair" in February and March of 1956 with the publication of the aforementioned *Southern Manifesto* (see Chapter Two). (Sometimes, metaphors just work out without much help!) What the juxtaposition of *Brown*

I and *Plessy* does show is the interplay among court decisions over the years and how common law isn't a guarantee of justice in the pursuit of a public-school education. Equity, rather, is in the hands of those most closely connected to students and of those most clearly invested in ensuring fairness in education.

Chapter 4
Equity? Who Says? The Influence of the Courts and Common Law—Part III

Can Unreliable and Unpredictable Still Be Consequential?

"History can't be reduced to one thing.... Recognize that things are complicated. To really accomplish anything meaningful and lasting, you have to understand the full complexity."

—Mark Whitaker[71]

Few examples are more illustrative of the seemingly fickle nature of the Supreme Court than two school cases that took place in the early-to-mid twentieth century, *Minersville School District v. Gobitis* in 1940 and *West Virginia State Board of Education v. Barnette* in 1943. While most educators are familiar with the outcome in *Barnette*, which gave constitutional protection to students refusing to recite the Pledge of Allegiance, its predecessor is a bit less well-known. The *Gobitis* case is, however, exceptionally important in contrast to the later decision in *Barnette*: the former focused mainly on religion; the latter on speech and, students' civil liberties, its influence felt to the present day.

The initial issue was this. William and Lillian Gobitis, students in Minersville, Pennsylvania, devout Jehovah's Witnesses, refused to salute the American flag in school. Although they respected the flag and loved their country, their actions reflected their belief that according to their faith, saluting the flag would be akin to bowing to a graven image—the image being the flag.

Both Gobitis children were expelled from school, a consequence of what the school board viewed as insubordination. Their father initially brought this suit "to be relieved of the financial burden" he entailed having to enroll his children in private schooling and desired an injunction that would permit his children to return to public school in Minersville.[72]

The U.S. District Court held for Gobitis, not relieving him of the financial burden, but agreeing that the children had a liberty right under the Fourteenth Amendment to attend public school. Judge Maris said in his opinion, "The enforcement of…requiring the flag salute by children who are sincerely opposed to it upon conscientious religious grounds is not a reasonable method of teaching civics, including loyalty to the State and Federal Government…."[73] And as the children's actions would not compromise "the public safety, health or morals or the property or personal rights of their fellow citizens"[74] in violation of the Pennsylvania Constitution, the court ordered that the children be allowed to return to public school and, respecting their religious beliefs, not be required to salute the flag.

It is interesting to know that up to this point, no fewer than five similar flag salute cases had been brought before the U.S. Supreme Court, and in each, the Court "found that the requirement of such a school exercise was not beyond the powers of the states."[75] *Gobitis* came to be heard by the Supreme Court because the District Court's decision differed from the decisions in these previous cases.

Justice Frankfurter, writing the opinion in the 8-1 Supreme Court decision in *Gobitis*, viewed the flag salute ritual as an act of national solidarity. Justice Frankfurter, a European emigree, has been described as believing that "in periods of wartime, national unity is the most important thing…. [H]e advocated subordinating civil liberties to the greater good."[76] In his opinion, Frankfurter writes:

It is not our province to choose among competing considerations in the subtle process of securing effective loyalty to the traditional ideals of democracy, while respecting at the same time individual idiosyncrasies among a people so diversified in racial origins and religious alliances.[77]

To go back to Mark Whitaker's quote at the start of this chapter, it is important to understand the full complexity of things. In terms of decisions that have come down from the Court, understanding the full complexity can be knowing what was happening in the world at the time of the decision. At the time *Gobitis* was decided, the United States had not yet entered World War II;

however, there was a growing awareness of what was happening in Europe and growing concern about communism. The fallout after *Gobitis* resulted in Jehovah's Witnesses' being perceived, in some places throughout the country, as unpatriotic—a tremendous misinterpretation of the decision but one that had devastating consequences which included violence against Jehovah's Witnesses, additional expulsions, and fines or legal action taken against parents now held responsible for their children's delinquency.[78]

By the time *Barnette*, also a case about students who were observant Jehovah's Witnesses refusing to salute the flag, reached the Supreme Court, the United States was fully involved in World War II. In a relatively short span of years, the Supreme Court overturned its previous ruling in *Gobitis*. Some justices who had previously been in the majority, said in their concurrence in *Barnette*:

Reluctance to make the Federal Constitution a rigid bar against state regulation of conduct thought inimical to public welfare was the controlling influence which moved us to consent to the Gobitis decision. Long reflection convinced us that although the principle is sound, its application in the particular case was wrong.... We believe that the statute before us fails to accord full scope to the freedom of religion secured to the appellees by the First and Fourteenth Amendments.[79]

Thus, in *Barnette*, one factor greatly influencing the Court against the school district was the Court's seeming disregard of the Gobitis children's right as students to freely exercise their religious beliefs—a right stemming from the First Amendment and brought to the forefront by influential religious periodicals and commentary of the day.[80]

This quick turn of events, from 1940 to 1943, was important for many reasons, not the least of which was that it illustrated the influence of the public sentiment of the times on jurisprudence. How could public sentiment that had resulted in violence against a group that had lost their appeal in one case now influence a decision in another case involving members of the same group, a decision that overturned the previous case?

Justin Driver in his book *The Schoolhouse Gate* noted that schools are the perfect setting for constitutional conflict because, among other reasons, "the cultural anxieties that pervade the larger society often flash where law and education converge."[81] To give this context in considering *Gobitis* and *Barnette*, it would be helpful to share what Justice Jackson wrote in his opinion in *Barnette* about the important role that school boards play in educating youth for citizenship. He spoke of the Fourteenth Amendment as protecting citizens against the State, which included boards of education. He acknowledged the responsibilities that the state might have—but affirmed that these responsibilities must be discharged "within the limits of the Bill of Rights." He went on to say:

That they are educating the young for citizenship is reason for scrupulous protection of Constitutional freedoms of the individual, if we are not to strangle the free mind at its source and teach youth to discount important principles of our government as mere platitudes. Such Boards are numerous, and their territorial jurisdiction often small. But small and local authority may feel less sense of responsibility to the Constitution, and agencies of publicity may be less vigilant in calling it to account.[82]

What had happened in the interim? For one thing, Section 7 of House Joint Resolution 359, approved December 22, 1942 (56 Stat. 1074, 36 U.S.C. (1942 Supp.) § 172). This Statute "prescribes no penalties for nonconformity" in saluting the flag, but "provides…civilians will always show full respect to the flag when the pledge is given by merely standing at attention, men removing the headdress…."[83] Today, this practice is known and accepted—but that is where it came from!

If this may appear to deviate from my theme of equity in public education, think again. Equity, though not widely mentioned by name in court opinions, persists through many points of entry—religion being just one. What these cases are intended to illustrate is the very unpredictable human nature of the Court. The impact and influence of history and public opinion render precedent unreliable. The impact of changing the minds of even a few justices—not to mention the decisions themselves—is, nonetheless, consequential.

The question remains who is really and truly responsible for public education. If talking about the institution itself, the following analysis will reveal that the answer volleys between the schools, the courts, and a variety of outside influences, in many ways only peripherally connected to education, if at all. Going more deeply within the schoolhouse gates, however, tells a slightly different story if we let it.

First, some groundwork. Never forget that the U.S. Supreme Court justices are, and always have been, political appointments. With no constitutional guarantee of impartiality in decisions and no code of ethics (at least until efforts were made to initiate one in 2023), partisanship could be no surprise. For example, a piece of Supreme Court trivia reveals that the last Chief Justice appointed by a Democratic President was Chief Justice Fred Vinson—the Justice who unexpectedly died after failing to achieve consensus in the initial deliberations on *Brown I* during the 1950s. Does that imply that every Supreme Court decision since that time has been more conservative than liberal? Or that justices' future decisions can be predicted based on their past? Not necessarily so. You may recall my mentioning in a previous chapter that Justice Hugo Black had been a member of the Ku Klux Klan, a membership that he renounced prior to becoming a justice. Yet he is well-known for his opinions supporting civil rights, separation of church and state, freedom of the press, and, despite his dissent in *Tinker*, free speech.[84]

Looking at the Supreme Court over the years, defined through the legacies of its Chief Justices including and since *Brown*, shows insightful patterns. It is somewhat easy to identify which cases directly involve public education and which issues predominate during particular decades. More challenging, however, is determining whether certain judgments work for or against public education. This makes it almost a necessity to dive into the nuances of the justices' opinions and dissents.

For example, one of the more recent Supreme Court decisions in *B.L. v. Mahanoy Area School District* resulted in a favorable ruling for the student regarding disciplinary actions related to her use of Snapchat. It marked the first time the highest court gave some definition to the constitutional perimeter of the schoolhouse gate regarding social media. While the district may have lost the battle, do districts in general now benefit from knowing the limits? Or would districts be better off having the flexibility to work within the vagueness of undefined territory? Would students be better off? It's all a matter of perspective and timing.

Recent rulings in *Carson v. Makin* and *Kennedy v. Bremerton* that addressed public funding for religious schools in Maine and prayer by a coach on the football field immediately following a game, respectively, would beg the argument that the Supreme Court is treading in areas where it has no business and will become as Justice Frankfurter warned in *Gobitis*, "the school board for the country."[85] It has become clear that the right of public schools to operate without First Amendment establishment clause protection is tipping the balance between free exercise and concerns for safety and between public presence in school operations and the ability of those trained and entrusted by local school boards to fulfill their responsibilities.

Should judges stay out of the schoolhouse? Many would wish to see Justice Frankfurter's jurisprudence persist over time; still others would caution that if that were the case, the potential for violations of personal liberties would exponentially grow. This could happen if the local bias of each community influenced the interpretation of constitutional rights with more homogeneous populations potentially compromising diversity in practices and points of view. One only needs to read the headlines.

The takeaways from this perspective of the courts' influence on education are severalfold:

- It is important for educators to stay abreast of legal developments potentially affecting public education. Follow the press coverage carefully, taking note of media outlet bias. A great free source to consult is https://mediabiasfactcheck.com.

- When an article contains a link, don't hesitate to follow it as it may lead you to the original source of the information, which is always the most reliable place to look—even if you don't agree with the content!

- Recognize that while it is most important to follow the law as prescribed by the courts and by the legislature, there is tremendous latitude in every law's interpretation. That is where state statutes and codes, district policies, and school handbooks come in. The law takes many forms. For this reason, always remember that your role is *not* to practice law. Think twice and seek advice!

- Finally, and perhaps most importantly, recognize that as educators, you have the agency to be "creatively compliant" while working within the law. Mind the boundaries of your district policies and handbooks—but think about the unique ways you can make a difference.

Chapter 5
Equity? Who Says? What We Carry Within Ourselves

"You can't go back and change the beginning, but you can start where you are and change the ending."
>—James R. Sherman, also attributed to C.S. Lewis[86]

Social psychologist Claude Steele writes in *Whistling Vivaldi* that "everyone is capable of bias.... We are not, and cannot be, all-knowing and completely objective. Our understandings and views of the world are partial and reflect the circumstances of our particular lives."[87] Recognizing that one is both capable of and guilty of bias is an important factor contributing not only to our views on equity but also to our ability to grant equity to others in the daily pursuit of living. That is why bias is essential to consider in any study about equity.

Our biases are influenced not only by the times in which we live but also by the attitudes of those who came before us—those from our families, our communities, and even those beyond our immediate reach in our government and greater society. Biases reflect how we feel about ourselves and others and how others may feel about us—and our *perceptions* of how others feel about us.

The term "bias" often carries with it a negative connotation—to be biased against. Even though one can be biased *toward* something in a good way, the hostility associated with the use of the term to show, explain, or justify discrimination is the more common usage of the word and is apt to induce a damaging and visceral response.

It is a difficult thing to admit what might be viewed as a personal failing whether by others or in our deepest private feelings about ourselves. Doing so reveals vulnerability. Our efforts to hide that of which we may be ashamed or conflicted often end up in the creation of a new reality for ourselves and those around us. This new reality is, in essence, a fiction that can make it difficult to see people and circumstances clearly, for who and what they really are.

Dara Horn, in her book *People Love Dead Jews*, illustrates how this type of fiction operates when she speaks to the circumstances under which many Jews chose to change their names. While one would not immediately associate this practice with bias in that it is not necessarily a negative inclination toward *another*, it does reflect what merriam-webster.com refers to as "an inclination of temperament or outlook"[88] that results from a judgment one makes. Viewed in this way, the practice of name-changing is actually a form of what Horn talks of as a way of hiding from bias to survive. She says, "These people [who changed their names] were not 'self-hating Jews.' They were simply staring down a reality that they could not deny."[89]

One can speculate that name-changing resulted, and still results today, if people feel they lack the courage to fight societal realities or are helpless in being unable to assist themselves or others in the face of discrimination. While that may, in part, be the case, name-changing also derived from a felt need to protect future generations by trying to ensure greater opportunities for success and a good life in one's new country. Indeed, this was likely the case in my own family when my uncle, who trained as a dentist, changed his name from "Pedlosky" to "Peddie" in hopes that the change would cause people to regard him differently as a professional.

Keeping that in mind, it is essential to base what we know about people on what they, themselves, reveal to us, and on what we can learn about different cultures through primary and secondary sources. This is important to understanding how bias develops and why it can be so difficult to erase. For example, what we learn from Horn in her book is that interestingly, name-changing at Ellis Island didn't really happen the way many have been led to believe because, among other things, immigration officers, many who spoke the language of arriving immigrants or benefited from the help of translators, relied on ship manifests for the proper spelling of people's names.[90] And even though people's experiences coming through Ellis Island remain legendary, this was not necessarily the case in reality. Despite the fact that my family did emigrate from Russia, for example, my uncle's changing of his name did not take place when he emigrated but afterward.

Looking at bias per Merriam-Webster as an inclination in outlook resulting from a judgment one makes is revealing. Using the example of Ellis Island, for many, initial optimism about coming to America ultimately resulted in the realization that all was not what they had hoped it would be. This is, unfortunately, a reality for many immigrants both coming into a new country or even resettling from different parts of the same country—immigrants in their own land. Myths form and are passed down for self-preservation and with the best of intentions. While these stories can contribute feelings of innocence and protection rather than malice, they can also contribute to bias as people lose themselves to a reality where there is no guarantee of fitting in.

What can one take away from this illustration about bias in general?

First, while the reasons behind bias may often be motivated by malevolence, bias can be driven by innocuous but important needs such as survival, belonging, and the desire to create understanding or acceptance. It can also be the unintended consequence of ignorance.

Second, bias has its own sustaining power. It is certainly understandable that mythology could come from a desire to instill hope and create a mindset for success in any challenging and potentially life-changing situation.

Third (and certainly not last), bias is taught—both intentionally and unintentionally. Again, I go back to Horn's work because the example is so vivid. She explains that the only thing many people know about Jews is what they have learned from their social studies books—that Jews are people who got murdered in the Holocaust. And, while people in the Jewish community clearly promoted teaching the Holocaust curriculum and many states have legislated it, if that is the only way people know Jews, they receive a distorted view of culture and civilization.[91]

In essence, what we teach can instill and perpetuate bias—it is really an education problem. Similar logic to that described above regarding Holocaust studies can be applied to the study of Black History. Although it is extremely important, if the only understanding most people have of Black History is that Africans and African Americans were enslaved, tremendous injustice is done to black people, to African culture and civilization, to African American folk culture, and to the greater society that includes people of all races. Teaching history, any history, from only one perspective or moment in time, freezes that history, removing it from lived experience. Doing so compromises a most valuable part of any school curriculum, of any person's education—that which helps develop an appreciation for each individual's uniqueness and what they contribute to the world and to our democratic society.

What lessons does this look at personal bias and "what we carry within ourselves" teach as we go about creating opportunities for equity in our classrooms and schools? Let's consider the following:

- We need to educate, as Dara Horn has suggested, for curiosity.[92] Many people want to help fight bias, but they either don't know what help is needed or how to channel their efforts.

- Being aware of situations where there is bias brings clarity. It is important to let that clarity carefully guide our way forward because it is so difficult to unsee things once one sees them. (Think about the judge saying to a jury, "disregard that statement." How many times have you then, sarcastically, said to yourself, "Sure they will!")

- Let's flip the narrative. How can we encourage students to think about living in a manner that regards people as human and not as symbols? Doing so encourages curiosity and helps reduce or eliminate distortion.

- Rather than co-opting history and marginalizing living people, it is necessary to connect with others in ways that facilitate sharing the richness of their cultures—to find ways to say, "you're speaking my language," so that people understand it is not only possible but extremely important to have empathy for others who are different from themselves.

Chapter 6
Someone Else's Party:
A Reflection on Culture

Someone else's theater party.
You are welcomed in.
But as the night goes on,
You wonder if, when you join in the laughter,
you are laughing for the same reason.
Or whether asking the person in front of you to remove his hat
Will offend or be understood.
So you apologize.

True story. I thought I was simply buying tickets to see a play. Instead, quite unintentionally, I had signed up for the cultural experience of a lifetime.

My husband and I attended a wonderful play on Broadway called *Skeleton Crew* written by the fabulous Dominique Morisseau—of Detroit. Perhaps I should have been alerted that there was going to be more to our evening than simply enjoying the play when, waiting for the theater doors to open, we were met by TV reporters covering this particular evening's performance. Why? We couldn't imagine as everyone in line was simply standing there, in the rain, waiting to enter. Nothing appeared to be different from any other night at the theater—except, of course, the impromptu interview set with lights and microphones we then noticed just beyond the doors and under the marquis.

One reporter approached us. Oh, why did we make eye contact? Then the questions. "What made you want to see this play?" he asked. "Was there an actor in particular that you were hoping to see?"

"Oh," I replied, "We're here for Broadway Week, and we thought it would be a great story—and of course, we wanted to see Phylicia Rashad." Little did we know that the play, itself, was only Act 1.

At 8:00, curtain time came and went, but still the lights did not go out. Life was positively swirling around us!

Asking questions, we learned that this night's performance was a celebration of Detroit and that people had come from all over to rejoice in the success of one of Detroit's own! One of the best lines from all the speeches that evening came from the show's director who said something to the effect of, "I grew up in Detroit, went to school in Detroit. I may not have learned much about Shakespeare, but I did learn about my people."

And, as I watched reunion after reunion among those in this most impressive gathering of New York City and Broadway's elite including African American actors, directors, writers, athletes, and more, I grew increasingly aware that I had stepped into something unique and tremendously special. It was special not only because of those assembled but even more because watching and listening gave me a window into a wonderful world I was fast realizing I knew so little about. And *that* is the purpose of including my story here.

I have never been to Detroit. My only connection to the city has been through the two very significant legal challenges linked to it—*Gary B.* and *Bradley*, as well as its role as an endpoint in the Great Migration. Here, in the midst of what I had only known as a city from which the white population fled and whose inner-city schools ill-equipped black students for a competitive world, came such sparks of life, hope, and the dignity of accomplishment. There was such a demonstration of pride in not only being black but in coming from Detroit.

What does this have to do with equity in schools? Well, just about everything. The evening taught me, among other things:

- How important it is to recognize the uniqueness of *everyone's* culture and to try to understand the vastness of cultural differences by being a willing, objective, and conscientious observer.
- Not to be afraid to ask questions, even if it appears that everyone else already knows the answers. What they know may be quite different from any answer you may assume.

- That space is important for the ability it provides to be seen, heard, and viewed on one's own stage—no matter where that stage is or what one is doing on it.

- How important it is not to be judgmental or to assume answers before you know them—or that you have accurately assessed a situation.

- How equity does *not* hold the same meaning for any two people, much less for any two cultures—and that it is very often difficult to learn about the equity needs of another in due time to address those needs. This is why it is so important to ask questions, to be a keen observer, and to encourage others to communicate.

- While in New York visiting museums and monuments, I was seeking illustrations to make connections with equity in education based on what I had read about the exhibits. I learned that looking too hard sometimes doesn't give you what you expect and can make you miss the serendipitous things happening around you. Sometimes, what you are looking for isn't where you thought you would find it. Sometimes, it finds you, and that's when making the connection is the sweetest.

It is a great experience being at "someone else's party"—alone or in a group where you find yourself in the observable minority. As educators, we are always learning—and the world is the best classroom! You can be part of "the smaller half" in so many ways. Race, ethnicity, religion, sex, or gender most readily come to mind. However, there are others.

Consider, for example, attending a gathering of professionals other than educators; accompanying a friend to something they have done before, but you have not; traveling to a place where you are not a native speaker; attending a celebration where you do not know anyone except for the celebrant; or volunteering in your community, perhaps at a senior care home. You have quite likely been in many of these situations throughout your life.

But, when you do in the future, look around, and survey how people are interacting and what is unique and special about the setting and their needs. Make a conscious effort to think about how you feel in that setting, how you are responding to what is happening around you, whether you have any unique needs or accommodations that would help you feel more comfortable, and what the group is doing to make you feel included. These types of experiences are great starting points for creating equity in schools. They bring sensitivity to differences and to the very human need to be seen, to be understood, and to be accepted.

All in all, I was SO grateful that our interview never made it to the 11:00 news! My comments, while honest and true, were totally inadequate to the privilege of being part of something greater and a most inspiring evening!

I end this chapter by sharing (and adding to) excerpts from a note that *Skeleton Crew's* playwright, Dominique Morisseau, included in our Playbill, and that she has given permission for me to include here. She calls these "Permissions for Engagement," and I think her title and ideas translate well to the consideration of expressions of equity in the education setting. Here they are, with her permission and with my additions in parentheses.

Consider this an invitation to be yourselves in this audience (classroom).

You are allowed to laugh audibly (though, respectfully, and not at others).

You are allowed to have audible moments of reaction and response.

This is also live theatre and the actors need you to engage with them in a way that doesn't distract or thwart their performance. (Again, apply to your classroom.)

Please be an audience member (learner) *that joins with the village, either silently or vocally, in support of the journey we will take collectively. Exhale together. Laugh together.*

This is community.[93]

Chapter 7
You Say Equity—You Say Equality—
I Say BOTH!

In some circles, people would argue that "equity" is a more politically correct goal and one that is more achievable than "equality." I beg to differ. Who wouldn't want to support the need for those kids of various heights to stand on differently sized boxes in order to look over the fence at the ball game? I certainly can relate as I would easily have been the shortest child! And, in this scenario at least, having a box that doesn't accommodate one's height is like having no way at all to see the game.

However, this example is as unrealistic as it is simplistic. While one could argue the blatant unfairness of *equity* in providing access to see a ballgame over the fence to one child and not the other smaller children, perhaps the bigger issue in this situation is one of *equality*—why each of those children didn't have the money to buy a ticket to see the game from inside the fence in the first place. Should the fact that the children pictured in that image are all children of color make a difference? Everything depends upon context.

As an avid theatergoer, I've always thought it completely unfair that the taller patrons aren't provided tickets only for the seats at the back—especially as the tallest ones always seem to end up in front of me! Of course, that would be a tremendous disservice in *equity* to the ones accompanying them who wish to enjoy the experience together. Whose rights prevail? My right to enjoy a production to which I've purchased a ticket or the tall person's right to enjoy a production in the company of their family? Or how about the time I attended the New York revival of *Hair* and the *only* two attending in full costume, including huge wigs were—you guessed it—seated directly in front of me! Fairness and justice are not only related, but relative.

Equity and equality need to work in concert with one another. They must exist in the same space in time and on the same plane. They must each be facilitated with understanding and appreciation to know and/or anticipate the needs of others, the wisdom and creativity to find space for competing needs and interests to coexist, and the authority, whether assigned, imputed, or undertaken, to make both happen in the necessary proportions.

One of the basic differences between the two is that in its pure sense, equality should be easy to see, especially when it is lacking. Equity, as it is dependent upon so many variables, judgments, and circumstances, is much more challenging to discern and to effect. Even then, "equality" in the eye of the beholder has, in many cases throughout history, been more like who will get the bigger half than a truly equal share.

The difficulties in defining those terms are not made any easier by reading the Supreme Court decisions. The Court often speaks in terms of equality as regards school cases in desegregation and funding, their opinions focused on "equal" protection as assured by the Fourteenth Amendment. When the word "equity" is used, the Court refers to legal terminology meaning justice and fairness, less as a goal but more in a procedural sense, such as how civil cases or cases in "equity" (which includes many challenges relating to education) seek to address wrongs against victims using injunctions, actions, or some type of restorative compensation rather than punitive measures such as incarceration used in criminal trials.

Swann v. Charlotte-Mecklenberg Board of Education was one of the important desegregation cases following *Brown*. In his opinion on this issue that set the standard by authorizing the use of busing to achieve school desegregation, Chief Justice Warren Burger added a bit of substance to help us understand "equity." He wrote that "to do equity" entails

> *mould[ing] each [court] decree to the necessities of the particular case. Flexibility, rather than rigidity, has distinguished it. The qualities of mercy and practicality have made equity the instrument for nice adjustment and reconciliation between the public interest and private needs as well as between competing private claims.*[94]

He further says, "words are poor instruments to convey the sense of basic fairness inherent in equity. Substance, not semantics, must govern...."[95]

So from where does our expectation of equity rather than equality stem? Most likely from our experience as educators with legislation passed through Congress aimed at ensuring children, and sometimes adults, receive support for those attributes that make them unique and that may require more custom tailoring than a one-size-fits-all approach to education.

What immediately comes to mind are some pieces of legislation passed by Congress with which you may be familiar from your work in schools: the Individuals with Disabilities Education Act, Section 504 of the Rehabilitation Act of 1973, the Americans with Disabilities Amendments Act of 2008, Title VI of the Civil Rights Act of 1954, Title VII of the Civil Rights Act of 1964, and Title IX of the Education Amendments Act of 1972.

As with Chief Justice Burger's description of equity, in helping schools meet the unique needs of students and staff, these pieces of legislation *do* mold recommended solutions to fit "the necessities of the particular case." They *do* seek "adjustment and reconciliation" between the "public interest," or what resources the school can offer and the "private needs" of each individual. And it is always hoped that "mercy and practicality" are the driving forces in each conversation that is had, each relationship that is formed, and each decision that is made.

But, if the courts are more interested in "equal" than "equitable," how do their rulings affect our practices in education? Court judgments matter directly to those acting as plaintiffs and defendants. Decisions from the U.S. Supreme Court and certain other higher courts are considered precedential, meaning they absolutely influence the decisions of other courts below.

The interpretation and staying power of those decisions in the years that follow, especially with momentous cases such as *Brown*, can vary greatly based upon social mores, personal biases, politics, and how justices view their role in interpreting past court opinions and the Constitution, itself. For example, justices calling themselves "originalists" will look to interpret the Constitution using the same sensibilities as the framers who wrote it. Others will view the Constitution and prior common law from the perspective of the world as it has changed, using it as a symbolic, malleable interpretation rather than as an unyielding template.

Thomas Jefferson's words related to jurisprudence bear consideration:

[L]aws and institutions must go hand in hand with the progress of the human mind. As that becomes more developed, more enlightened, as new discoveries are made, new truths discovered and manners and opinions change, with the change of circumstances, institutions must advance also to keep pace with the times. We might as well require a man to wear still the coat which fitted him when a boy as civilized society to remain ever under the regimen of their barbarous ancestors.[96]

Relative to education, there is always a question as to whether it is the proper role of the Supreme Court, or any court for that matter, to weigh in at all on decisions affecting school systems or individual schools. In *Gobitis*, when children were expelled after refusing to participate in the Pledge of Allegiance,[97] the U.S. Supreme Court ruled in favor of the school district with Justice Felix Frankfurter writing in his opinion, "'[T]he courtroom is not the arena for debating issues of educational policy'" and doing so would make the Court "'the school board for the country.'"[98] Frankfurter's words appeared to put a period on court involvement in education when he concluded that overruling the District's expulsions would impose "'pedagogical and psychological dogma in a field where courts possess no marked and certainly no controlling competence.'"[99]

Justin Driver speaks of *Gobitis* as "the fulcrum of modern American education law,"[100] reflecting the Supreme Court's complete turnaround from *Gobitis* to *Barnette* only three years later. From that time forward, courts, including and especially the Supreme Court, have weighed in on students' constitutional rights to the point that in 1969, in a case defining a student's rights to free speech, the Supreme Court opinion in *Tinker v. Des Moines* proclaimed, "It can hardly be argued that…students…shed their constitutional rights to freedom of speech or expression at the schoolhouse gate."[101]

So is it significant that the Supreme Court has not introduced the idea of "equity" in many of its judgments related to education? I believe it depends upon how much emphasis one places on the influence of the Court on schools—which has varied over time.

This is not to imply, however, that the Court is or should always be eager to jump in to play that role. After many years of speculation as to when the Supreme Court would decide a case having to do with schools and social media, for example, the justices finally did in 2020, with the case of Brandi

Levy against the Mahanoy Area School District[102] again affirming students' rights to this type of free speech, under certain conditions.

The issue of equality rather than equity in schools and, indeed, in society as a whole, seems to take center stage in the years before *Brown*. At that time, equality was defined largely by provincial attitudes toward race and influenced by the Supreme Court decision in *Plessy v. Ferguson* that validated "separate but equal." The decision and dissent in *Plessy* are a great example of how justices' opinions and dissents illustrate the push and pull of the court as it debated the meaning of "equality."

One might read some irony into the words of Justice Henry Billings Brown, who wrote the majority opinion in *Plessy*. He said at first:

The object of the [Fourteenth] amendment was undoubtedly to enforce the equality of the two races before the law,[103]
To which he added:

...but in the nature of things it could not have been intended to abolish distinctions based upon color, or to endorse social, as distinguished from political, equality.... If one race be inferior to the other socially, the Constitution of the United States cannot put them upon the same plane.[104]

The power of the Court came through in the use of those words, and the criteria Justice Brown set for equality was the deciding factor in subsequent cases, giving legal clout to a racial hierarchy. Justice John Marshall Harlan was the only one to dissent in *Plessy*, yet his words, "Our Constitution is color-blind, and neither knows nor tolerates classes among citizens"[105] wielded much power ultimately leading up to *Brown*. He may have been one voice, but that voice mattered.

Aligning with Justice Brown's expression of societal mores at the time, great liberties were taken with the presumption of equality—liberties that have been the source of much *inequity* and differential treatment, particularly among white people and people of color, and poor people and those of means. When people were assigned to separate railway cars, the subject of *Plessy v. Ferguson* in 1896, it would have been terribly incorrect to understand "separate but 'equal'" as meaning either equality of accommodations or equality in the treatment of passengers on train cars.

One of the "colored" Pullman cars has been on display at the National Museum of African American History and Culture in Washington, D.C. Walking through it reveals the lack of luggage racks and smaller bathrooms than would be found in the "white" cars.[106]

Another difference would have been in the location of the cars—those furthest from the smoke and noise of the engines reserved for more privileged white passengers. Passengers of either black or mixed race who wished to move into the "white" cars were able to do so in some states but needed to retreat to "colored" cars when passing over other state borders.

When *Brown I* attempted to address "separate but equal" in schools, despite outlining the specific obstacles to addressing such inequities in *Brown II*, the Supreme Court revealed a fatal flaw in its inability to gather the entire country behind this unanimous decision. The Court's decisions as they evolved both before and after *Brown* may lead one to question fairness and justice coming from court rulings and how much anyone can really become invested in what has been decided.

The decision in *Brown* may, in fact, mark a shift from the pursuit of equality to a consideration of equity. After 1954, various state and federal courts posed ongoing challenges to the call for school desegregation; the Civil Rights movement awakened a level of social activism in the interest of treating people as people rather than as members of a favored or unfavored group. And beginning in the 1970s, Congress enacted legislation to address the unique needs of those with disabilities. All of this followed the *Brown* decision, some common law rulings appearing to grow more nuanced with subtle calls for *equity* in an effort to build a common ground for living together.

Of course, that doesn't mean those efforts were successful, as so many structures to ensure "separate but equal" after the Civil War fought against opportunities for people of all races to live together. These vestiges of the past, including things like redlining that continue to make it so very difficult for people of color to acquire mortgages or even feel welcomed into many neighborhoods, convince me it is still necessary to consider *both* equity and equality—side-by-side, especially in schools.

As much as the domestic diaspora brought African Americans north and west in an effort to escape the horrors of slavery, a reverse migration is actually taking place today with black northerners moving south, frustrated by an inability to thrive as their ancestors had hoped. Is this leading us back to "separate and (un)equal" with segregated communities seeking to retreat into stereotypical attitudes that had been baked into societal mores for centuries?[107]

As long as there is any danger of this happening, and the courts, including and especially the Supreme Court, have shown this is eminently possible, we must ensure that everyone is operating on an even playing field *and* that we explore the meaning of equity as it can help us facilitate what Margaret Wheatley in *Leadership and the New Science: Discovering Order in a Chaotic World* calls "webs of interconnections that weave the world together."[108]

Unlike equality, which by its very nature almost implies an even exchange of goods, equity is more of an understanding, more intangible. Isabel Wilkerson in *Caste* speaks about something she calls "radical empathy." She defines this as "putting in the work to educate oneself and to listen with a humble heart to understand another's experience from their perspective, not as we imagine we would feel."[109] What makes this especially important as applied to education is that it requires us to connect as people—to engage in an affirmative act.

Justice Burger's words about equity in 1971, flexibility, mercy, and reconciliation, echo Wilkerson's idea of radical empathy.

Judge Learned Hand was a highly esteemed judge on the U.S. Court of Appeals for the Second Circuit. In 1944, he delivered a speech, "The Spirit of Liberty," where he reflected on the idea of liberty reinforcing the need for equity and equality in the way we treat our children so that they can be the stewards of the future. His words echo Wilkerson's radical empathy when he says, "[T]he spirit of liberty is the spirit which seeks to understand the mind[s] of other men and women…the spirit which weighs their interests alongside its own without bias…."[110]

Bearing in mind Judge Learned Hand's words about how the spirit of liberty values all beings, as well as Chief Justice Burger's guidelines for "doing equity" and Isabel Wilkerson's "radical empathy," consider the following as questions we can continue to explore relative to our students and ourselves, especially in the school setting:

- How can we encourage others to openly share their perspective about an experience?
- How can we develop listening skills that show we are fully engaged and open to what others have to say?

- How can we demonstrate flexibility when faced with challenges?
- How can we be practical in our choices while, at the same time, showing generosity, forbearance, and grace?
- What adjustments can we make to address both individual needs and the good of the whole?
- What are the parameters that we want to establish for a "just" society in our classroom, in our school?

Chapter 8
What Does It Mean to Receive an Equitable Education?

Investing solely in the decisions of our courts can lead one to ponder whether achieving equity in education is nothing more than Quixote-inspired idealism. Though some may deem it, to use a well-known idiom, tilting at windmills, those who believe it to be necessary will continue to press on knowing its value.

Achieving equity is as complex and nuanced as the term itself, influenced by the mores and the attitudes of those living at a specific moment in time. In his opinion in *Brown*, Chief Justice Burger identifies both an important aspect of this challenge—in that particular case to achieve equality—as well as what he believes needs to be done.

In approaching this problem, we cannot turn the clock back to 1868, when the [14th] Amendment was adopted, or even to 1896, when Plessy v. Ferguson was written. We must consider public education in the light of its full development and its present place in American life throughout the Nation.[111]

I agree with Chief Justice Burger that we cannot turn back the clock. I also believe it is difficult to move forward without an appreciation for what has brought us to this point in time. That is why I feel it is so important for educators to be aware of the legal framework I have outlined in this study so as to appreciate what it means for students to be afforded equitable opportunities in public education.

Knowing the stories and the struggles of those who have come before provides insight and guidance. So many times in my research I found myself making comparisons between the legal battles of the times and those we currently face. For example in the Reconstruction years before *Plessy*, equity in education for children regardless of race was a priority—so much so that it was actually inscribed in Louisiana's State Constitution in 1868. It is difficult to consider the issue of integration in our public schools without appreciating that the decision in *Brown I* was not the first of these battles—nor is it to be the last.

Ultimately, Homer Plessy's fight wasn't only about getting a seat on the train car of his choice. It was really, to draw from Langston Hughes once again, about getting a "seat at the table"—being accepted as a member of society and all that it entails. Homer Plessy and the members of the Citizens' Committee, or the Comité des Citoyens as it was known in New Orleans at the time, who staged Plessy's flagrant challenge to the Separate Car Act and his subsequent arrest, recognized the necessity of civil rights activism to secure equity.

Such activism was very much alive in Louisiana, even prior to the Civil War and before Homer Plessy was born, particularly in New Orleans. French and Spanish rule in that city had left behind a society of three races: white, black (predominantly slaves), and free people of color who enjoyed some, though not all, of the rights of the white race. At that time, integrated schools were part of New Orleans life, having evolved from a belief in and commitment to the importance of education for all children irrespective of race.

While public school integration and interracial marriage (which was also accepted at the time) are part of our hard-fought judicial heritage today, in a similar vein, they were among the societal institutions that became collateral damage at the end of Reconstruction when Supreme Court cases such as *United States v. Cruikshank* in 1876 challenged what some may have initially assumed about the reach of the First and Fourteenth Amendments.

The circumstances that led to *Cruikshank* involved a challenged gubernatorial election, after which violence erupted between newly enfranchised blacks and white supremacists seeking to return to pre-Civil War slavery. In what because known as the "Colfax Massacre," approximately 150 blacks were slaughtered by white rebels perpetuating what was thought to be yet another act of violence instigated by the Ku Klux Klan. The Supreme Court ruled in favor of the rebels, limiting the ability of the North to protect newly freed slaves and effectively resulting in an end to Reconstruction.[112] Some might argue, however, that efforts to assure rights to newly freed slaves continued up to the decision in *Plessy* in 1896.

While this story may leave you scratching your head in wonderment about how *Cruikshank* has any connection to public school equity, the ruling in the case leaves no doubt. First, this case redefined the reach of the 14th Amendment, which, conceived as a guarantee of equal protection and due process to citizens of the United States and the state of their residence, was now interpreted as applying only to state action and not action between private individuals. The fallout enhanced racial violence and greatly diminished rights for people of color. The 14th Amendment became an instrument of the state, increasingly fickle without providing the protections that could be afforded through federal uniformity.

In a similar vein, *Cruikshank* influenced interpretation of the First Amendment's right to assembly, the Colfax Massacre violence having begun as a peaceful assembly of black people challenging election results.[113]

Of course, what we have been considering up to this point is really "schooling," which is not necessarily the same thing as "learning" and "teaching." When thinking about the conditions that define equity, it is important to consider all three. For example, teaching without schooling has taken place under oppressive conditions and at great peril for both teacher and learner throughout history, including teaching slaves on plantations to read.

In his book *Deschooling Society*, Ivan Illich speaks to the relationship between learning, teaching, and schooling. "Teaching," he says, "may contribute to certain kinds of learning under certain circumstances.... Most learning happens casually, and even most intentional learning is not the result of programmed instruction."[114] How can equality be assured under these conditions where there is no baseline? In this example, it is much easier to think in terms of equity and how it can apply to learning as divorced from programmed instruction or what we would consider "schooling." This begs the following question: how heavily does learning depend upon life experience in proportion to opportunities that may be delivered in the schoolhouse?

Isabel Wilkerson illustrates this through the character of George Starling in her book, *The Warmth of Other Suns*. Starling, a black man, was deprived of a formal education by virtue of circumstance and destiny during the years of the Great Migration (1915–1970). He moved North, as did so many others over those decades, embracing a new life and a career riding the rails that provided him with broad perspective on what was happening in the world and to the people around him. Starling ultimately found his unique style as a learner, experiencing schooling from a much more expansive classroom than a traditional education could have afforded him.[115]

Starling's "seat at the table" was not in any way what he had hoped or expected it would be. As Wilkerson explains, "…the revolution that opened up the best in education…had come too late for him."[116] This reminds me of Chief Justice Burger's words in *Brown* shared earlier in this chapter when he spoke of the importance of considering public education "in light of its present place in American life throughout the Nation."

Perhaps what we envision as the ultimate, perfect, "real" education is more than what can be delivered in a schoolhouse—and needs to be more. This is something to keep in mind as we continue to consider the meaning of equity.

Equality would imply that everyone receives the same books, the same competence in teachers, and the same conditions under which to attend school. Books and materials can be measured—but what about teachers and something as fluid as the conditions under which students learn? How can they be measured? Would we even want to?

The manner in which we meet the needs of children identified under the Individuals with Disabilities Education Act (IDEA) brings up what some feel is one of the more obvious distinctions between equality and equity in public education. Students who qualify under the IDEA are provided with an education program tailored to enable them to make progress in light of their unique circumstances (*Endrew F. v. Douglas Cty. Sch. Dist. RE—1*, 580 U.S. ___ (2017)). Required is not a change to a school's curriculum but, rather, accommodations that afford students access to that curriculum. Is this reminiscent of the children standing on various-sized boxes outside the chain link fence surrounding the ballfield? What do you think?

This type of equity is assured under federal legislation passed by Congress and originally signed by President Ford as the Education for All Handicapped Children Act in 1975 (Public Law 94–142), with adaptations made by Supreme Court decisions since that time, most recently in the case of *Endrew F. v. Douglas County School District* in 2017. The original legislation opened the door for students who are unable, for a variety of reasons, to process information in the way that many students manage to process information and access learning opportunities. This type of equity is important because public education is a uniform system based, in large part, upon a homogeneous culture.

On the surface, therefore, achieving equity among a consistent population, with certain prescriptive accommodations to create that consistency, should be easy—in fact, "equality" should be very much achievable in that world. But the reality is that public education serves a *generic* "public"—a public that brings with it a plethora of differences that form the essence of what it means to be human. For that very reason, public education can never truly be equal as each person who participates, every different stakeholder, comes from a different starting point and employs a different system to process the world around them.

Dara Horn stresses how important it is to develop an appreciation for differences by cultivating curiosity. She notes, "Living in a pluralistic society is about curiosity, about human differences....Our role if we're educating people should be to be educating them toward curiosity."[117] I would contend that Horn sets forth an important trajectory, where an important step toward achieving equity is engaging that curiosity to explore and embrace the possibilities inherent in our similarities and our differences.

These similarities and differences are important to creating an equitable *culture*. According to Horn, societies "impose their identity from the outside in."[118] School cultures are no different. Author Ladlee Hubbard from the Harvard Radcliffe Institute would agree, saying that the margins of a society help to shape the center, its coherency, and the way in which the center perceives itself.[119] The similarities and differences among us help define the margins of that society.

Equitable education, thus, evolves from the uniqueness of its learners and may include the following:

- Creating a framework identifying areas of significance for all learners which, in turn, helps define the culture of the school
- Ensuring that those "areas of significance" reflect an appreciation for past history, present society, future trajectories, and possibilities
- Finally, considering what makes each learner a "person who matters" including, but not limited to, giving each a voice within a culture that values their stories, their similarities, *and* their differences

Chapter 9
Where Do We Go from Here?

"Get up, boy," Rosa Parks said to Keith. "Your name is Plessy. You have work to do."

—Amy Nathan[120]

Perception and belief do not guarantee reality. What would happen if you woke one morning to find that you were not who you imagined yourself to be? Many probably don't give it much thought and go about living life as their own design based upon the past. However, sometimes artifacts surface to challenge that design.

Phoebe Ferguson grew up the daughter of politically liberal parents in New Orleans only to discover many years later that she was, in fact, the great-great-granddaughter of a judge responsible for institutionalizing Jim Crow discriminatory practices that lasted for decades (and, some would argue, are even present today) across the South and parts of the North. Judge John Howard Ferguson's ruling in 1892 almost single-handedly ended the hopes brought on by Reconstruction that former slaves and people of color would be recognized with the rights afforded to other U.S. citizens.

Coming to terms with that reality, Phoebe and Keith Plessy, Homer Plessy's first cousin, three generations removed (K. Plessy, personal communication, October 16, 2023), joined as Plessy *and* Ferguson to teach about this history and to stimulate conversation about equity.[121] Their actions speak to the human desire to connect and the resilience that is possible when people are willing to confront the past and look toward the future.

This is not an easy thing to do. It is difficult to come face-to-face with the past—especially if it is not what you believed it to be. It is uncomfortable at best. But it is important to look the past squarely in the face in order to deal with what it has left behind in its aftermath.

When awakening to a past that brings surprise or discomfort, people often don't understand what it means or what to do about it. Plessy and Ferguson put their pasts to righting a wrong—one of the most virulent, harmful, and ill-decided Supreme Court decisions in our history.

Similarly, Charles Taney, a great-great-great nephew of Chief Justice Roger Taney, delivered, in 2017, an apology to one of Scott's descendants, Lynne Jackson. Chief Justice Taney was responsible for the horrific 1857 decision in *Dred Scott v. Sanford* that determined blacks were not to be considered U.S. citizens and took control of slavery out of the hands of Congress. The current Mr. Taney was quoted in *The Baltimore Sun* as saying:

'Apologizing to the Scotts for the Dred Scott decision is like bringing a Band-Aid to an amputation. It's right and necessary to apologize, but what's important now is what actions we can all take' to bring about racial reconciliation in America.[122]

Both Taney and Jackson are in discussions about what to do with the statues of the notorious Justice Taney, considering which to remove and which should stay in place. It is being contemplated that those statues that remain be offset by statues of Dred Scott and other notable historic figures, such as Frederick Douglass and Harriet Tubman, to inspire "ongoing 'dialogue' about matters of racial reconciliation and justice."[123] There is, of course, a substantial cost to removing a statue and then storing it, and many opinions to consider in determining which, when, and where. Perhaps the most important message coming from this reconciliation though, is from Charles Taney who noted that "any reconciliation is three-part: an apology for injuries, forgiveness from the victims, and the creation of a new foundation of trust."[124]

The most significant word here may, in fact, be "trust." In its meaning lies the answer to the question how do we talk about equity when we *can't* talk about equity—or when we're too uncomfortable doing so? Or, perhaps, the question should really be how do we talk about equity when we can't talk about *equality*—or when we're too uncomfortable doing so? Remember back to the comment made by a colleague of mine that I referred to earlier in this book—something's being equitable is a concession to its not being equal.

Equity is so important that it just makes common sense. Perhaps that's why it is so hard for people to break it down and analyze what it takes to achieve it. It's second nature.

Equity is the proverbial "elephant in the room." Is that because people feel helpless in their ability to work toward achieving it? Is it because people feel uncomfortable based on their own personal feelings about equity or experiences with equity? Or is it, among other things, because it is so difficult to put a pin in exactly what equity is in education or anywhere else for that matter?

My expectation was that this would be a very short book you could carry about rather than only store on a library shelf. I hope its deliberately brief exploration of case law has provided insight into how and why courts have or have not supported equity in public education. It is essential that we are aware of the impact that actions taken by the courts and various other stakeholders have on schooling. It is, thus, my hope that when people see this book, they will recognize this and be able to talk about what can be done based upon creative compliance with the law and the inspiration of their own stories, whomever they wake up and find themselves to be.

To that end, I conclude this formal study with an introduction by sharing evolving perspectives on equity in public education from those living the challenge every day of their professional lives—the results of inquiry made through surveys and conversations with students, colleagues, and interested educators across the country.

One question I asked was for individuals to share words or phrases they associated with equity in public education. To date, in over 100 responses, these words or phrases most often came to mind:

- Empowerment
- Diversity
- Safety
- Attention to biases that may exist
- Equal access
- Equal opportunity
- Resources necessary to achieve both access and opportunity
- Fairness

- Personalization/recognition of differences
- Tailoring support to meet individual needs
- Justice

These terms and phrases, based upon details expressed in the individual responses, can be juxtaposed in a manner such that, for example:

- Equal access + equal opportunity depends upon the resources necessary to achieve both access and opportunity.
- To achieve fairness + personalization and the recognition of differences, there needs to be a tailoring of support to meet individual needs.
- The implication that the implementation of all these words and phrases associated with equity in public education ultimately leads to justice.

Other survey questions asked respondents to share how they implemented equity practices in their classrooms and/or schools. I encourage you to not restrict your reading of what follows to any one specific topic of survey responses. Many responses cross over categories. All provide inspiring ideas and pathways—and are especially insightful. Educators represent 19 states, all age groups, and years of experience in the field, as well as a wide range of professional assignments K-12 with the vast majority being teachers. Every effort has been made to reproduce information as supplied by respondents with any alteration reflecting a need for clarity not impacting the integrity of the response.

With regard to implementing equity-focused programs or initiatives in *curriculum*, the following are among the responses received:

- Creating a rubric to evaluate curricular materials through an equity lens.
- Moving away from a "one-size-fits-all" assessment mentality, which automatically puts some students at a disadvantage.
- Recognizing the unique cultures of students, incorporating values and perspectives from underrepresented communities with the goal of developing background knowledge, deepening understanding, engaging in effective discourse and debate to reach new conclusions

about complex concepts and topics, cultivating cultural pride and ownership, and recognizing cultural contributions to global development.

- Students have access to online materials and textbooks; they are provided with laptops and Wi-Fi Hotspots.
- Adding lots of choice, interest, and skill-based initiatives in literacy instruction to try and cultivate joy and to help students identify as readers and writers as they grow skills.
- Differentiating content, process, and product depending on the needs of the students.
- Making myself, as the teacher, available to provide additional assistance or guidance to students who need it; setting up opportunities for more advanced students to help their struggling peers.
- Actually following IEPs and 504 plans.
- Standards-based grading, sustainability standards, group assessment, performance assessment, and open note assessment.
- Creating a podcast to share stories related to curriculum, culture, relationships, classroom and school organization, resources and materials, and staffing. Guests have provided insights into all those areas.
- We no longer purchase curriculum. Our learners are the curriculum. We look at community and global problems that are authentic and meaningful to each learner. The learners can follow their interests and passions, breathe, and go for depth.
- Lesson material and teacher expectations are adjusted to fit the ability of the student.
- Working toward the representation of diverse people in curricular materials.
- In science, we have made intentional steps to represent non-Western euro-centric perspectives and contributions. We have also incorporated opportunities to consider how systemic racism has influenced discovery and research in science.
- Students on the autism spectrum are given their own music period at the elementary level, which allows students to explore instruments on their own and incorporate their IEP goals into my lessons (e.g. sharing materials).

- I was an Ethnic Studies teacher who deliberately chose a curriculum to expand upon dominant narratives taught in the classroom. I taught my students how to see dominant narratives that maintained status quo or power structures and how to look for resistance and transformative narratives around them and in their own lives. Students became the authors of their own stories and not only chose their own projects and learning but assessed their own work.

- Differentiated materials and topic choices are reflective of students' individual strengths, preferences, needs, and so on.

- Personalized pathways at all levels; no "grades" based on date of manufacture in the elementary levels as students are grouped in multiage classrooms.

- Differentiating content (objectives and information), process (materials and tasks), and product (expectations). Tomlinson and Universal Design for Learning (UDL) providing multiple means of engagement, representation, actions, and expression. This means I must find ways for students to meet the course objectives and succeed.

- Having lesson objectives for multiple abilities.

- Stories and read-alouds.

- Through the use of choice boards of similar type activities, students can often choose their pathway of learning to include specific topics (or avoid them).

- All literature must be diverse in topic as well as author. Diverse reading material. Allow for textbooks to be geared to a variety of reading levels. They all look the same but the reading levels are different. The student doesn't know the difference.

- Budgeting focus on providing the resources (such as Kindles) that students need AT HOME to ensure that they are provided equitable opportunities to continue school-wide expectations, such as completing homework, outside of the classroom.

- Having a wide range of books in the classroom library allows for all students to feel represented in literature and also doing my best to make sure test questions are not biased toward any one culture.

- Getting all students 1:1 access to laptops during and after the pandemic; providing summer reading books.

- We continue to make sure our learners have the resources and materials at all times that they need. In connection to technology, every learner has a 1:1 device and in addition, we provide Hotspots for our learners who are unable to afford Wi-Fi in their homes.

- Providing differentiated materials and topic choices reflective of students' individual strengths, preferences, needs, and so on and sharing resources and promoting genuine dialogue in areas that have been identified as challenging, sensitive and/or controversial.

- Regardless of socioeconomic status, all resources and materials used in school are provided free of charge (including meals).

- Providing materials leveled to match students' needs and abilities, When I taught in an elementary school: tools such as scissors for left and right-handed students, or ensuring vision testing to secure glasses for visually challenged students, or at the university, loaning books to those who did not have student loan yet to buy the book, or securing the book online for students to use.

With regard to implementing equity-focused programs or initiatives in *culture*, responses included:

- A great deal of work here has been accomplished with my work on disproportionality in schools. Also, the anti-bullying legislation has demonstrated that certain groups are targeted, which has opened up eyes to how different groups are treated.

- Inquiry-based instruction will be used throughout content areas to drive student curiosity, critical thinking, analysis, discovery, and new understandings for students. By promoting engagement and experimentation, students will learn how to critically analyze, develop questions, and engage in problem-solving. In addition, inquiry protocols will drive school-based decisions within the school community; teachers will analyze student data to develop instructional next steps to give students plentiful opportunities to demonstrate proficiency in standards. Professional learning communities will also engage in the inquiry process, assessing student growth on a larger scale and adjusting curriculum and instructional goals to best meet student needs.

- My classrooms celebrate multiple holidays and let students lead discussions around traditions they celebrate with their families.
- Professional development around Zaretta Hammond, *Culturally Responsive Teaching and the Brain.*
- As a school, we attempt to implement equity-based initiatives, but we struggle with accountability/old-school metrics and our ideal of restorative practices.
- I hold a social skills group where students are presented with problems or situations that challenge them to come up with varied solutions from varied perspectives.
- My classroom is a "safe haven" for many of the students. They treat it like a second homeroom where they can come during lunch to practice or come before school to get some work done or practice their instruments. All of my students are welcome, and none are put out.
- I've tried to include perspectives [from] those who are LGBT+ and religious minorities in the curriculum.
- The opening unit of my year asks students to build a model of transdisciplinary thinking. We examine the strengths and weaknesses of math, science, philosophy, and art and apply that to the climate change problem. I also try to incorporate as much indigenous knowledge as possible throughout the year.
- I have facilitated professional development relating to leaders' beliefs about equity.
- We are continually working to move away from a deficit model to help open opportunities for all students to participate in all levels of academic rigor.
- Our alternative students could take my course for college credit (Ethnic Studies 101) which reframed their own experiences of school and learning. When students see themselves as empowered (in addition to the very real marginalization they experienced), their opportunity to challenge their victimization shifts dramatically. Our students often came from generational poverty and addiction as well as sickness or disability, and my school community gave our students the opportunity and tools to understand how those positionalities impacted their thinking, responses, and ability to negotiate school and

the world around them. Instead of victims, our student body was a community of survivors.

- Providing opportunities for my students to challenge historical perspectives.
- Student voice and choice in most school-wide endeavors/initiatives.
- Providing a safe environment for successful learning, acceptance, and appreciation. I try to create a classroom as a community of learners, all supporting each other through professional learning communities (PLC).
- I tried to include respect for different cultures as a positive—we are all diminished when everyone is measured by "our" standards.
- As a community nonprofit, our programming is school based in arts education and inclusion.
- Using broad references for all examples.
- "Welcoming schools" trainings for staff and team meetings.
- Initially, I focused on connecting the students to each other and the larger world. This was through class discussion and short writing responses that were structured to focus on commonality. The ultimate goal was empathy.
- Students are provided with an opportunity to define the class culture which may fluctuate between classes. These self-defining activities around classroom culture and expectations help ensure all students have bought into the expectations and are willing/able to achieve them.
- Multicultural texts.
- We significantly altered the faculty composition by adopting a philosophy that we were recruiting teachers who mirrored the student population. It was a little easier in high school and middle school, but we have done a good job, with more work to do at the administrative level.
- Focus on hiring staff that are representative of the community where students will attend. It is imperative that students see themselves within those who are helping them be the best version of themselves.
- Actively recruiting at least 50% staff of color in the final selection pool. Stay conversations and incentives to work on retaining staff of color.
- Non-discrimination clause is strictly followed.

- Providing staff trained and willing to meet student needs and abilities. I chaired and served on search committees to select faculty who were aware and willing to help students succeed beyond just conducting classes.

- As an administrator, I tried to help see that our staff looked like our students—not always easy when trying to balance all qualities that a candidate had to offer—especially since we were always challenged by trying to attract minority candidates to our rural KY school.

With regard to implementing equity-focused programs or initiatives in *relationships*, responses were as follows:

- This is a challenge, especially in top-down systems. I incorporated protocols that put systems in place to gather diverse perspectives. It should be done more at the student level.

- There are no set rules for equity in my classroom—it tends to happen organically. For example, if there are students who tend to monopolize the time of the teacher (always first to answer, always seeking attention), it falls upon the teacher to give the other students, who are overshadowed, opportunities to contribute.

- In keeping with its Whole Girl educational approach, the school's curriculum weaves together social and emotional learning and academic knowledge and skills to ensure that girls and gender-expansive youth take leadership, collaborate effectively, appropriately assert and support their opinion, and develop a critical lens for analyzing power dynamics that exist in the intersection of gender, race, and other signifiers. These practices will be evident throughout the curriculum in service of the school's mission.

- Focal student approach to increase students within the sphere of success.

- We claim to use restorative processes and we focus quite a bit on building relationships, but we struggle to implement and end up often using the language of relationships and restorative justice to uphold inconsistent or low academic expectations.

- I build relationships with all of my students. I am mindful of each student's culture and life experiences.

- Essentially this is the same as culture. I help my students establish a group dynamic where the band is like a family. The students enjoy spending time together and helping each other. It did take a few years to build this dynamic.

- Modeling teaching, Problem Posing education (*Pedagogy of the Oppressed*), grit, grappling.

- In the area of our Portrait of a Graduate, we work on citizenship to make sure everyone receives what they need and how they need it. This is also getting connected in our Mastery Transcript. We help find resources to help students get the resources to overcome any challenges.

- In addition to staff involvement in our equity initiatives, we are also joining professional collaborations around culturally responsive pedagogy and gender/racial equity in science (STEP UP Physics & Women in Science Programs).

- In my course, our mantra was: "How does your positionality bias your epistemology?" Our students were taught how to see our differences as that of circumstances and culture, not intrinsically bad or wrong. We highlighted our connections to each other as well as our differences from which we could understand and learn. We also practice mindfulness and how to recognize trauma responses in order to better negotiate our own stumbling blocks. We saw ourselves as family and confronted the inherently hierarchical nature of traditional schooling.

- Sharing resources and promoting genuine dialogue in areas that have been identified as challenging, sensitive, or controversial.

- Consequences for undesirable actions are tailored to individual needs when appropriate.

- Providing opportunities for connecting with students in various ways and among themselves. I provide my cell number and office hours with time before, at lunch, or after class to meet with them individually. I tried to attend special events they were in as well as serve as the advisor for the honorary. I started the academic year with each of the class and me writing a biographic statement and creating a picture collage that was combined into a class book with each member of the class took home to read one night.

- Social skills groups and partnerships.
- Social skills groups and social stories.
- Using the students' personal experiences rather than purchased resources. I also used copies of original documents.

With regard to implementing equity-focused programs or initiatives in *classroom organization*, responses included:

- The actual furniture and school renovation projects have all included student voice. We have flexible and realistic timelines for homework and assessments and put the teachers on a timeline that requires them to return student work in a respectful timeframe.
- Standards-based grading with plentiful opportunities for revision supports goal-setting, self-reflection, portfolio building, ownership, and meta-cognitive skills—all of these pieces are grounded in equity best practices because they focus on the individual functional level of students (while holding high expectations that all students can grow and succeed), rather than a "one-size-fits-all" belief.
- Desks set up for group discussion and collaboration.
- I try to offer choice and provide lots of differentiation, especially in modes of expressing ideas, and strong relationships/focus on assets. I have a long way to go to truly create a student-led classroom.
- I include students in the creation of classroom rules and procedures. I work at a virtual school, so I do not have a physical classroom.
- Actually following IEPs and 504s in regard to preferential seating, use of microphones, and so on.
- Decentralized seating, student choice, student art, flexible timelines, and link libraries.
- Periodically, students are seated in order for them to help each other. Often, a student can explain lessons more understandably than the teacher. Hearing and sight disabilities are addressed with seating near the front of the room.
- Equity can include flexible paging and varied demonstrations of mastery for students with a range of talents and gifts while working toward a common set of criteria.

- All students have access to flexible seating in my classroom; however, I only have 5 flexible seating options for an average class size of 25 so it is not available to all if every student requested flexible seating.
- We sat in a circle. Students had the opportunity to work with and sit with someone new each day. Students scored their own work on a proficiency-based model. All students were seen as experts in their own lives and learning.
- Flexibility with assignment due dates when needed. Alternate choices for assigned tasks. Alternate venues for seminar meetings.
- Inclusion for all students of all abilities.
- Organizing the classroom so students can work together in groups or pairs, or alone, and have access to varied seating, desks, and technology. I have seated students with auditory or visual difficulty accordingly. For example, I worked with deaf students and their ASL assistants or auditory transcribers to place them where they can follow the lessons.
- Working with everyone.
- Differentiation surrounding different abilities.

With regard to implementing equity-focused programs or initiatives in *school organization*, responses were as follows:

- I completed disproportionality studies by each core department. I tracked students from 8th grade through 12th grade. I followed students from 8th grade to their course sections in general, honors, and AP courses and by race, ethnicity, gender, special ed., and so on. We changed entry criteria for courses that precluded many groups. We eliminated prerequisites, an unbelievable gatekeeper. We also studied the students who got into pre-algebra in 6th grade and noticed it lacked girls and students of color.
- A block schedule will provide students with longer periods of time in Math and ELA. A block schedule also allows for classes to vary in their order throughout the week so that students receive the mandated seat minutes in all of their classes. The research supports that increased learning time promotes greater Math and Literacy achievement.

- School schedule overhaul—building in consistent time for intervention and enrichment, expanding opportunities for social studies, science, and electives, programming for multiple pathways toward graduation in high school and partnering with community colleges for bridge programs, time in days for teachers to collaborate on planning and discussing student work, PLCs.
- Again, we claim to practice restorative justice and attempt to execute but we are a work in progress.
- The science department has eliminated prerequisites for advanced courses. Over the past 10 years, this has created the most diverse student population in Honors and AP courses at the school.
- Gender-neutral bathrooms available.
- Creating opportunities for students and families to participate in experiences together.

Survey respondents also shared *challenges* they have faced with equity, including practices that they viewed as not resulting in the desired outcomes.

- I'd say that individuals can keep problems in place by implementing strategies of comfort—things that keep the most people happy (adults). People tend to pick and choose items to implement and that is a challenge. The students, in some places, are receiving the benefit but I find that adult beliefs can get in the way. For example, not all adults agreed with eliminating the ridiculous prerequisites in science and came to a board meeting and said we were going to regret it!
- Like anything, I struggle to execute at 100%, but I think I stick with ideas and execute with fidelity.
- I think this question is missing the idea of scale. There are committees and the like that we have implemented at the school, but they have not addressed the problem fast enough, in my opinion.
- Despite no prerequisites, we continue to see lower enrollment in science courses among our Black and Latinx communities. Additionally, the percentage of women in AP Physics is disproportionately low.
- Learning Language Disability students push into music classes in order to have equal access to music as their general education peers.

However, it is difficult because a general classroom size is 20 students plus 13 learning language students. This means I now have 33 students and it is difficult to manage (behaviors and not enough materials), everyone misses out on quality instruction which to me cancels out the equity part.
- We tried to make it a practice of looking for minority candidates, but this was often very difficult.

I hope you will consider the results of my research and my survey and conversations as jumping off points for ideas that can be tailored to the particular nature and needs of your classroom, your school, and the children with whom you work. They can also provide support for you in meeting unexpected challenges and in coming to terms with your own experiences with and ideas about equity in public education. My hope is that you will find and share inspiration from a diverse group of fellow practitioners and that you will take something valuable from your reading. Please take advantage of opportunities to engage in ongoing dialogue about this most important aspect of our lives and of our children's education!

Notes

[1] Smith (2021), p. 78.

[2] Sunstein (2004).

[3] Sunstein (2004).

[4] Chodas, ed. (2003).

[5] Hughes (n.d.).

[6] Reynolds & Kendi (2020), p. 183.

[7] 7 (1966) The Black Panther Party Ten-Point Program (n.d.).

[8] Reynolds & Kendi (2020), p. 150.

[9] Williams (1984), n.p.

[10] S. Allen, personal communication (January 1, 2022).

[11] Baldwin (1993), p. 18.

[12] Smith (2021), p. 183.

[13] U.S. Const. art. III, § 2.

[14] National Park Service (2021), fn 5.

[15] National Park Service (2021).

[16] National Park Service (2021).

[17] See the Smithsonian's National Museum of American History Behring Center for excellent resources relating to these cases at https://americanhistory.si.edu/brown/history/1-segregated/separate-but-equal.html

[18] *Avery C. Alexander Act* (2006).

[19] Rojas (2021).

[20] Duncan-Smith (2022).

[21] Thomas (2021).

22 *Gong Lum v. Rice* (1927), at 82.

23 Alvarez (1986).

24 Alvarez (1986).

25 Arevalo (n.d.). See also
http://almalopez.com/projects/ChicanasLatinas/mendezfelicitas1.html and the
National Archives Educator Resources at
https://www.archives.gov/education/lessons/mendez-case for more
information about this case.

26 Arevalo (n.d.).

27 *Brown v. Board of Education of Topeka* (1954), at 495.

28 *Brown v. Board of Education of Topeka* (1954), at 493.

29 *Brown v. Board of Education of Topeka* (1955), at 300.

30 *Brown v. Board of Education of Topeka* (1955), at 300.

31 *Brown v. Board of Education of Topeka* (1955), at 300.

32 *Brown v. Board of Education of Topeka* (1955), at 300–301.

33 *The Southern Manifesto* (1956).

34 *The Southern Manifesto* (1956).

35 *The Southern Manifesto* (1956).

36 *San Antonio Independent School District v. Rodriguez* (1973), at 10.

37 *San Antonio Independent School District v. Rodriguez* (1973), at 24.

38 *San Antonio Independent School District v. Rodriguez* (1973), at 24.

39 *San Antonio Independent School District v. Rodriguez* (1973), at 28.

40 Kinlaw (2020). (To note: One of the best places to find information about
this case including many primary resources is at *The Public School Forum of
North Carolina*, https://www.ncforum.org/leandro/. It helps develop an
understanding of what North Carolina is doing to implement the
recommendations of the court and the difficulties involved in doing so.)

41 Education Law Center (February 7, 2023).

42 A comprehensive history of this on-going litigation can be found at
https://edlawcenter.org/litigation/abbott-v-burke/abbott-v.-burke-
overview.html

43 *Abbott Overview* (n.d.).

44 Wilkerson (2011), p. 378.

45 Wilkerson (2011), p. 244.

46 Wilkerson (2011), p. 190.

47 World Population Review (n.d.).

48 Jonathan Kozol, in his book *Savage Inequalities,* speaks to racial inequities in the schools of East St. Louis. The history and impact of the St. Louis Arch is also worth exploring. And, if you happen to be visiting Kansas City, Missouri, insight into the history of that city's neighborhoods can be experienced through a 90-minute GPS-linked audio tour found on an app called "Voice Map." This is a free tour, "Dividing Lines: A History of Segregation in Kansas City."

49 *Milliken v. Bradley* (1974).

50 More information about redlining in Detroit can be found at https://www.canr.msu.edu/redlining/detroit.

51 *Gary B. v. Whitmer* (2020), p. 2.

52 *Gary B. v. Whitmer* (2020), p. 4.

53 *Gary B. v. Whitmer* (2020), p. 49.

54 *Gary B. v. Whitmer* (2020), p. 60.

55 Dickens (1859), p. 1.

56 Kierkegaard (c1843).

57 Milestone Documents: Plessy v. Ferguson (1896).

58 Luxenberg (2019), p. 13.

59 *Davis v. County School Board* (1952) at 339.

60 *Davis v. County School Board* (1952) at 340.

61 United States Senate, *Hugo Black Investigation*, July 11, 1935.

62 Chang (2022).

63 *Trump v. Hawaii* (2018), Section IV D.

64 Kapur (2021), p. 270.

65 *Brown v. Board of Education of Topeka* (1954), at 494–495.

66 Kapur (2021), p. 271.

67 *Brown v. Board of Education of Topeka* (1954), at 493.

68 Kapur (2021), p. 295.

69 "Ridiculous Anti-Climax" (1955), p. 2.

70 Kapur (2021), p. 315. More about this fascinating story and turn of events can be found in Kapur's book, chapters 10–12.

71 Whitaker (2023).

[72] *Minersville School District v. Gobitis* (1940), at 592.

[73] *Gobitis v. Minersville School District* (1938), at 273.

[74] *Gobitis v. Minersville School District* (1938), at 274.

[75] *West Virginia v. Barnette* (1943), at 664.

[76] Peters (2007), p. 762.

[77] *Minersville School District v. Gobitis* (1940), at 598.

[78] Peters (2007), p. 762.

[79] *West Virginia v. Barnette* (1943), at 643.

[80] Driver (2018), p. 7.

[81] Driver (2018), p. 10.

[82] *West Virginia v. Barnette* (1943), at 637.

[83] *West Virginia v. Barnette* (1943), at 643.

[84] Pacelle (n.d.).

[85] *Minersville School District v. Gobitis* (1940), at 598.

[86] James R. Sherman in *Rejection* also attributed, likely inaccurately, to C.S. Lewis.

[87] Steele (2010), p. 14.

[88] https://www.merriam-webster.com/dictionary/bias.

[89] Horn (2021), p. 93.

[90] Horn (2021), p. 90.

[91] Horn (2022).

[92] Horn (2022).

[93] Morisseau (n.d.), shared with permission from the author.

[94] *Swann v. Charlotte-Mecklenberg Board of Education* (1971), at 15.

[95] *Swann v. Charlotte-Mecklenberg Board of Education* (1971), at 31.

[96] Jefferson (1816).

[97] *Minersville School District v. Gobitis* (1940).

[98] *Minersville School District v. Gobitis* (1940), at 598.

[99] *Minersville School District v. Gobitis* (1940), at 597.

[100] Driver (2018), p. 8.

[101] *Tinker v. Des Moines Independent Community School District* (1969), at 506.

[102] *Mahanoy Area School District v. B.L.*, 594 U.S. ___ (2021).

[103] *Plessy v. Ferguson* (1896), at 163.

[104] *Plessy v. Ferguson* (1896), at 163.

[105] *Plessy v. Ferguson* (1896), at 163.

[106] Palmer (2016).

[107] A great resource on this topic is Taylor, K., Frankenberg, E., & Siegel-Hawley, G. (2019). Racial Segregation in the Southern Schools, School Districts, and Counties Where Districts Have Seceded. AERA Open, 5(3). https://doi.org/10.1177/2332858419860152; https://journals.sagepub.com/doi/full/10.1177/2332858419860152

[108] Wheatley (2005), p. 158.

[109] Wilkerson (2020), p. 386.

[110] Hand (1944).

[111] *Brown v. Board of Education of Topeka* (1954), at 492–93.

[112] Committee of 70 & United States House of Representatives (1874–1875).

[113] A great explanation of *Cruikshank* and perspective on its impact can be found at https://harvardcrcl.org/wp-content/uploads/sites/10/2011/09/385_Pope.pdf

[114] Illich (2000), p. 12.

[115] Wilkerson (2011), p. 532.

[116] Wilkerson (2011), p 420.

[117] Horn (2022).

[118] Horn (2022).

[119] Hubbard (2022).

[120] Nathan (2021), p. 143.

[121] See the Plessy and Ferguson Initiative for more information at https://www.plessyandferguson.org

[122] Pitts (2017).

[123] Pitts (2017).

[124] Pitts (2017).

References

Abbott I, 100 N.J. 269 (1985) through Abbott XXIII, 241 N.J. 249 (2020).

Abbott Overview. (n.d.). Education Law Center. Retrieved July 6, 2022, from
    https://edlawcenter.org/litigation/abbott-v-burke/abbott-v.-burke-
    overview.html

Alvarez, Jr., R. (1986, Spring). The Lemon Grove incident. *San Diego
    Historical Society Quarterly*, **32**(2).
    https://sandiegohistory.org/journal/1986/april/lemongrove/

Arevalo, L. (n.d.). Letter to Felicita Mendez.
    http://almalopez.com/projects/ChicanasLatinas/mendezfelicitas6.html

Avery C. Alexander Act, La. Stat. tit. 15 § 572.9 (2006).
    https://casetext.com/statute/louisiana-revised-statutes/revised-
    statutes/title-15-criminal-procedure/chapter-5-reprieve-pardon-and-
    parole/part-i-reprieve-and-pardon/section-155729-avery-c-alexander-act-
    application-process

Baldwin, J. (1993). *The fire next time*. Vintage International.

BlackPast.org. (n.d.). *(1966) The Black Panther Party Ten-Point Program.*
    BLACKPAST. https://www.blackpast.org/african-american-history/black-
    panther-party-ten-point-program-1966/

Brown v. Board of Education of Topeka, 347 U.S. 483 (1954).

Brown v. Board of Education of Topeka, 349 U.S. 294 (1955).

BlackPast.org. (n.d.). *(1966) The Black Panther Party Ten-Point Program.* BLACKPAST. https://www.blackpast.org/african-american-history/black-panther-party-ten-point-program-1966/

Chang, R. [@KorematsuCtr]. (2022, January 30). *He lost at U.S. Supreme Court. Opinion of the Court, authored by Justice Hugo Black, stated powerfully that* [Tweet]. Twitter. https://twitter.com/korematsuctr/status/1487827025628827651?s=21&t=MRpycZXzNNP41UmfR8u8nA

Chodos, A., ed. (2003). *Circa January 1961: Lorenz and the butterfly effect.* APSNews. Retrieved March 9, 2023, from https://www.aps.org/publications/apsnews/200301/history.cfm

Committee of 70 & United States House of Representatives. (1874–75). *Colfax Massacre Reports* (Yenor, S, Ed.). Teaching American History. Retrieved July 17, 2022, from https://teachingamericanhistory.org/document/colfax-massacre-reports/

Cumming v. Richmond County Board of Education, 175 U.S. 528 (1899).

Davis v. County School Board, 103 F. Supp. 337 (E.D. Va. 1952).

Dickens, C. (1859). *Charles Dickens Quotes.* The Charles Dickens Page. Retrieved July 8, 2022, from https://www.charlesdickenspage.com/charles-dickens-quotes.html

Driver, J. (2018). *The schoolhouse gate: Public education, the Supreme Court, and the battle for the American mind.* Vintage Books.

Duncan-Smith, N. (2022, January 10). Louisana (sic) governor pardons central character in historic 1896 Plessy v. Ferguson 'separate but equal' case; Descendant says 'a truly blessed day for my ancestor.' *Atlanta Black Star*. https://atlantablackstar.com/2022/01/10/louisana-governor-pardons-central-character-in-historic-1896-plessy-v-ferguson-separate-but-equal-case-descendant-says-a-truly-blessed-day-for-my-ancestor/

Education Law Center (2023, February 7). *A historic victory for petitioners in school funding lawsuit* [Press release]. https://www.elc-pa.org/wp-content/uploads/2023/02/Fair-Funding-Decision-Press-Release.pdf

Endrew F. v. Douglas County School District, 580 U.S. ___ (2017).

Gary B. v. Whitmer, Nos. 18-1855/1871 (6th Cir. 2020). https://www.opn.ca6.uscourts.gov/opinions.pdf/20a0124p-06.pdf

Gobitis v. Minersville School Dist., 24 F.Supp. 271 (E.D. Pa. 1938).

Gong Lum v. Rice, 275 U.S. 78 (1927).

Hand, L. (1944). *The spirit of liberty* [Speech]. FIRE. https://www.thefire.org/first-amendment-library/special-collections/the-spirit-of-liberty-speech-by-judge-learned-hand-1944/

Horn, D. (2021). *People love dead Jews: Reports from a haunted present.* W.W. Norton & Company.

Horn, D. (2022, February 8). *Women on the move: Dara Horn* [Webinar]. The Temple Emanu-El Streicker Center. https://streicker.nyc/past-event-recordings/2

Hubbard, L. (2022, April 27). *The descendants (a novel)*. Harvard Radcliffe Institute [Webinar]. https://www.youtube.com/watch?v=2V3O86U1LjA

Hughes, L. (n.d.). *I, too*. Poets.org. Retrieved July 7, 2022, from
    https://poets.org/poem/i-too

Illich, I. (2000). *Deschooling society*. Marion Boyars Publishers Ltd.

Jefferson, T. (1816). [Quotation]. Thomas Jefferson Memorial Southeast
    Portico, Washington, D.C.
    https://www.nps.gov/thje/learn/photosmultimedia/quotations.html

Kapur, G. (2021). *To drink from the well*. Blair.

Kierkegaard, S. (c1843). *Quotes*. Shmoop. Retrieved July 17, 2022, from
    https://www.shmoop.com/quotes/life-can-only-be-understood-
    backwards.html

Kinlaw, R. (2020, February 3). *What is Leandro?* (Video and Video
    Transcript). EdNC.

Luxenberg, S. (2019). *Separate: The story of Plessy v. Ferguson, and
    America's journey from slavery to segregation*, W.W. Norton &
    Company.
Mahanoy Area School District v. B.L., 594 U.S. ___ (2021).

Milliken v. Bradley, 418 U.S. 717 (1974).

Milestone Documents: Plessy v. Ferguson (1896). (n.d.) *National Archives*.
    Retrieved September 18, 2023, from https://www.archives.gov/milestone-
    documents/plessy-v-ferguson

Minersville School District v. Gobitis, 310 U.S. 586 (1940).

Merriam-Webster. (n.d.). *Merriam-Webster.com dictionary*. Retrieved July
    17, 2022, from https://www.merriam-webster.com/

Morisseau, D. (n.d.). *Permissions for engagement.* A note from the
playwright. A Playbill insert for Skeleton Crew.

Nathan, Amy. (2021). *Together.* Paul Dry Books.

National Park Service. (2021, November 4). *The Sarah Roberts Case.*
https://www.nps.gov/articles/the-sarah-roberts-case.htm#ftref5

Pacelle, R.L. Jr. (n.d.). *Hugo Black.* The first amendment encyclopedia.
https://www.mtsu.edu/first-amendment/article/1310/hugo-black

Palmer, A. (2016, June 13). This segregated railway car offers a visceral
reminder of the Jim Crow era. *Smithsonian Magazine.*
https://www.smithsonianmag.com/smithsonian-institution/segregated-
railway-car-offers-visceral-reminder-jim-crow-era-180959383/

Parents Involved in Community Schools v. Seattle School Dist. No. 1, 551
U.S. 701 (2007).

Peters, S.F., Peterson, G., Prettyman Jr., E., Boskey, B., Edmonds, G. (Fall
2007). Recollections of West Virginia State Board of Education v.
Barnette. *St. John's Law Review.* 81(4), Article 2.
https://scholarship.law.stjohns.edu/cgi/viewcontent.cgi?article=1191&con
text=lawreview

Pitts, Jonathan M. (2017, March 7). Roger Taney, Dred Scott families
reconcile 160 years after infamous Supreme Court Decision. *The
Baltimore Sun.* https://www.baltimoresun.com/politics/bs-md-scott-taney-
reconciliation-20170306-story.html

Plessy v. Ferguson, 163 U.S. 537 (1896).

Reynolds, J. & Kendi, I.X. (2020). *Stamped: Racism, antiracism, and you.*
Little, Brown and Company.

Ridiculous Anti-Climax (1955, October 26). *The Daily Tar Heel.*
    https://newspapers.digitalnc.org/lccn/sn92073228/1955-10-26/ed-1/seq-2/

Rojas, R. (2021, November 12). Homer Plessy's arrest in 1892 led to a
    landmark ruling. Now he may get justice. *The New York Times.*
    https://www.nytimes.com/2021/11/12/us/plessy-ferguson-pardon.html

San Antonio Independent School District v. Rodriguez, 411 U.S. 1 (1973).

Sherman, J.R. (1982). *Fact check: Did CS Lewis give this advice on starting
    over?* CHECKYOURFACT. Retrieved July 17, 2022, from
    https://checkyourfact.com/2019/07/26/fact-check-cs-lewis-cant-go-back-
    change-beginning-start-ending/

Smith, C. (2021). *How the word is passed.* Little, Brown and Company.

The Southern Manifesto, 84th Cong. Second Session, 102 Cong. Rec. part 4
    (1956, March 12).
    https://resources.saylor.org/wwwresources/archived/site/wp-
    content/uploads/2011/02/The-Southern-Manifesto.pdf

Steele, C. (2010). *Whistling Vivaldi.* W.W. Norton & Company.
Sunstein, C. R. (2004, April 25). Did Brown matter? *The New Yorker.*
    https://www.newyorker.com/magazine/2004/05/03/did-brown-matter

Swann v. Charlotte-Mecklenberg Board of Education, 402 U.S. 1 (1971).

Thomas, H. (2021, May 5). Before Brown v. Board of Education, there was
    Tape v. Hurley. *Library of Congress.*
    https://blogs.loc.gov/headlinesandheroes/2021/05/before-brown-v-
    education-there-was-tape-v-hurley/

Tinker v. Des Moines Independent Community School District, 393 U.S. 503
    (1969).

Trump v. Hawaii, 585 U.S. ___ (2018).

United States Senate. (1935, July 11). *Hugo Black Lobby Investigation.* https://www.senate.gov/about/powers-procedures/investigations/black-lobbying.htm

U.S. Const. art. III, § 2.

West Virginia State Board of Education v. Barnette, 319 U.S. 624 (1943).

Wheatley, M. (2005). *Leadership and the new science: Discovering order in a chaotic world,* (3rd ed.). Berrett-Koehler Publishers.

Whitaker, M. (2023). *Saying it loud: In conversation with Mark Whitaker and Eugene Robinson.* [Webinar]. Brennan Center LIVE. https://www.youtube.com/live/keEUSLJ30lY?feature=share

Wilkerson, I. (2011). *The warmth of other suns.* Vintage Books.

Wilkerson, I. (2020). *Caste.* Random House.

Williams, M. (1984). *The velveteen rabbit.* Running Press.

World Population Review. (n.d.). *Detroit, Michigan population 2022.* https://worldpopulationreview.com/us-cities/detroit-mi-population